IMAGES
of Rail

GREENSBORO
DEPOT

From Revolutionary War crossroads to today's crossing of major interstates, Greensboro has been long known as "the Gate City"—a nickname that was derived originally by our position along the mainlines of railroads. The Southern Railway system map is the main focal point in the main concourse and shows Greensboro as a railroad hub. This image was captured around 1976. (Courtesy of Mike Small.)

ON THE COVER: This is a 1955 view of the Greensboro Depot, now known as the J. Douglas Galyon Depot. It was completed in 1927 and still serves today as a train station and intermodal transit facility. It is also the home of the Greensboro chapter of the National Railway Historical Association. (Courtesy of the Greensboro History Museum.)

IMAGES
of Rail

GREENSBORO
DEPOT

David H. Steinberg and Kevin W. von der Lippe for the
Greensboro Chapter of the National Railway Historical Society

ARCADIA
PUBLISHING

ISBN 978-1-4671-0906-2

Published by Arcadia Publishing
Charleston, South Carolina

Printed in the United States of America

Library of Congress Control Number: 2023944874

For all general information, please contact Arcadia Publishing:
Telephone 843-853-2070
Fax 843-853-0044
E-mail sales@arcadiapublishing.com

Visit us on the Internet at www.arcadiapublishing.com

CONTENTS

ACKNOWLEDGMENTS

On behalf of the Greensboro Chapter of the National Railway Historical Society (NRHS), we would like to sincerely thank the Southern Railway Historical Association (SRHA) for its generous help. The association opened its archives to our research and generously allowed us to reproduce its photographs here. We would like to thank its president, Carl Ardrey; director of archives, George Eichelberger; Allyson and Kyle Shannon; and the entire group of volunteers. The SRHA's archives are located on the grounds of the Tennessee Valley Railway Museum in Chattanooga and are a treasure trove for the serious researcher. We are also grateful for the wonderful help provided by the Greensboro History Museum and its archivist, Elise Allison. Special thanks go out to all the members of the NRHS, and to our president R. Bruce Smith, Donald Arant, and Dr. Gene Lewis for their support of this book.

Unless otherwise noted, all images appear courtesy of the Southern Railway Historical Association.

INTRODUCTION

Greensboro's association with railroads commenced on January 19, 1849, when the North Carolina legislature's lower house passed a bill authorizing the construction of the North Carolina Railroad. As envisioned, this railroad was to operate from the town of Goldsboro via Greensboro to Charlotte. On January 25 of that same year, the measure passed the upper house to become law. Just two days later, by special act of the state legislature, the proposed North Carolina Railroad was incorporated. The railroad's creation was felt to be imperative by the state's lawmakers to allow for the opening of the Piedmont section of the state to trade and commerce in a way it could not otherwise be achieved. One stipulation was made, however: the state was ready to provide $2 million of the needed $3 million estimated cost to complete the project, on condition that the state's citizens come up with the remaining $1 million and that $500,000 be deposited into the company's treasury before actual work could commence.

North Carolinians must have realized the benefits a railroad tying the interior Piedmont section of the state with the eastern seaboard would provide. On June 5, 1850, John Motley Morehead, former governor of North Carolina and one of the railroad's most staunch promoters, announced that the stock had been subscribed for, scraped together literally dollar by dollar by the state's farmers, and work could now commence. These landowners were motivated greatly by the railroad's offer that those who purchased stock would be given preferential treatment when it came time to issue contracts for the line's building. Many of the adjoining landowners hoped to make an easy profit by building the railroad across their property.

Governor Morehead described the proposed railroad that would eventually operate from the state's east coast to its western mountains as "a tree of life for North Carolina." Of interest is the fact that as initially proposed, the section of the railroad operating from the state's capital to Charlotte was to run via a more direct and straighter route through Asheboro. The fact that Governor Morehead was a native of Greensboro surely assured the railroad would arc to the north toward his hometown.

Just a year later, on July 11, 1851, a parade formed on West Market Street and marched down South Elm to the site later occupied by the Clegg Hotel. It was the largest parade that had ever been held in the town. So large was the gathering that great difficulty was had controlling the masses. At a point near the site where the Elm-Davie underpass would later be built, the street was roped off and a select number of invited citizens were asked to go ahead of the crowd. It was reported that outside the ring were upwards of 20 people standing abreast. The occasion was to witness the beginning of the construction of the North Carolina Railroad. Shortly after 10:00 a.m., Governor Morehead, president of the new railroad, began his eloquent speech followed by remarks offered by Calvin Graves of Caswell County, who had cast the deciding vote in the North Carolina Senate that granted the railroad its charter.

Graves was an interesting individual. Hailing from Caswell County north of Greensboro, his constituents naturally wanted the new railroad to pass through their county. Graves, a realistic individual, knew that the railroad would never reach that far north. He therefore voted against his own county and subsequently lost the next election. In appreciation of what he had done and as a consolation to him, he was given the honor of turning the first shovelful of dirt for the line's construction. The dirt was then placed into a copper box along with the company charter and the names of the original subscribers to the building fund, along with newspapers and coins of the day, beside a scroll containing an address to be read on the 100th anniversary of the celebration. Immediately thereafter, the throng moved to a grove that occupied the site of what was destined in 1899 to become Greensboro's original Southern Railway passenger station on Buchanan Street, where a large barbeque had been prepared.

One

RAILROADS IN GREENSBORO

On June 20, 1852, the contract for the grading of the North Carolina Railroad was let. Construction was begun simultaneously at many separate locations along the route and not just by starting at one end. This was accomplished with numerous local contractors. A little over a year later, on June 23, 1853, actual track laying was underway at Goldsboro. It took an additional two and a half years, but the rails the entire length from Goldsboro to Charlotte were joined on January 29, 1856, at a place some five miles west of Greensboro now known as Hilltop. There, the two crews that had worked in opposite directions met and shook hands in joy. The speaker at the occasion was D.F. Caldwell, and with great formality, he had the pleasure of driving in the last spike. The two trains that had met at the joining both returned to Greensboro and pulled up to the Elm Street intersection where it had all begun seven years and two days before when the company was chartered by the state. The next day, the first trains, both passenger and freight, were in operation the full length of the line. The location of the 1857 passenger station that was built for the North Carolina Railroad was on the north side of the tracks on South Elm Street, near what is sometimes referred to as Hamburger Square.

With America's Civil War underway, On November 20, 1861, Confederate president Jefferson Davis recommended to the Confederate Congress that it was an absolute necessity that a railroad be built immediately from Greensboro to Danville, Virginia, to allow the South to have continued access to its Richmond capital. The existing line connecting Weldon with Petersburg, Virginia, had been captured by the North. On February 10, 1862, the Confederate Congress and the North Carolina legislature simultaneously approved the building of the line. It took only four months for the line to be ready, in May 1862.

On September 11, 1871, the original North Carolina Railroad was leased to the Richmond & Danville Railroad and then itself in receivership. This would remain the case until June 30, 1894, when the Southern Railway Company came into existence and assumed control of the Richmond & Danville.

North Carolina's northwestern counties were desirous of train service, so the 1868 North Carolina Constitutional Convention chartered the North-Western North Carolina Railroad. As envisioned, the line was to operate from some point off the existing North Carolina Railroad to the town of Salem. Later legislation authorized the road to extend either north to Mt. Airy or west to Wilkesboro and beyond. The company quickly organized, and by the end of April 1868, Cyrus P. Mendenhall, David F. Caldwell, and other influential Greensboro citizens had secured its eastern terminus for their town by agreeing to finance the grading as far as the Forsyth County line. In 1869, the North Carolina Railroad secured $20,000 of the new road's stock and arranged that a joint facility would be located at a point just west of Greensboro to be named Salem Junction. Unfortunately, the funds ran out before any track could be laid. Although the state offered its aid, the railroad felt there were too many strings attached, making it unacceptable to the company. North-Western North Carolina Railroad president Edward Belo in June 1870 proposed a merger with the North Carolina Railroad, but his terms were found to be unacceptable to the North Carolina Railroad stockholders. The North Carolina General Assembly then allowed the North-Western North Carolina Railroad to merge with any connecting road that would complete the track to Salem. Although the North Carolina Railroad was still interested, the Richmond & Danville Railroad (R&D) beat it to the punch. The R&D then acquired the North-Western North Carolina Railroad in early 1871, and on July 24, 1873, the first train operated the 29-mile distance from Greensboro to Salem (today's Winston-Salem) to become the third railroad to operate into Greensboro. In

1888, the line was extended another seven miles west. In early 1889, the line reached Donaha, and in 1890, the town of Wilkesboro was reached. In 1888, the owners of the line, the Richmond & Danville Railroad Company, extended the line to Bethania, and in 1889, the line was extended to Rural Hall to make a connection with the Cape Fear & Yadkin Valley Railway, the next railroad destined to enter Greensboro. This again can be attributed to the hand of John Morehead.

In 1852, the charter for the Western Railroad of North Carolina to extend from Fayetteville west through Cumberland, Moore, Harnett, and Chatham Counties was conceived but it was only able to build at that time to the coal mine area of Egypt, North Carolina, today better known as Cumnock. On February 25, 1879, the general assembly ratified an act allowing for the consolidation of the Western Railroad with the Mt. Airy Railroad, and the company's title was officially changed to the Cape Fear & Yadkin Valley Railway Company (CF&YV).

On April 6, 1881, the CF&YV entered into a contract with the Fayetteville & Florence Railroad to allow for extension over the graded roadbed of the CF&YV at that point and continuing on to the North Carolina–South Carolina state line. Simultaneous work pushed the line west so that trains were able to operate into Greensboro on the day of the company's annual meeting in 1884. By December 5, 1884, a total of 154 miles of right-of-way had been completed between Greensboro and Bennettsville, South Carolina.

In 1888, the CF&YV Railway constructed and opened its own passenger depot in downtown Greensboro. This station was on the south side of the tracks on Davie Street, about a block and a half from the original North Carolina depot. It remained in use until the Southern Railway acquired the Cape Fear & Yadkin Valley Railroad in 1899. Thereafter, it was demoted to freight service only. Construction expansion work then continued west from Greensboro, so that by July 20, 1888, excursion trains were able to carry thousands to the ceremonies for the completion of the mainline to the tiny hamlet of Mt. Airy at the foot of the famous Blue Ridge Mountains, which was now connected to the outer world. Two branch lines were then underway; one to Millsboro from the mainline at Factory Junction some 12 miles from Greensboro, and on December 28, 1888, the Madison, North Carolina, branch was in operation from the mainline at Stokesdale.

With the Panic of 1893 and the generally hard times of the era, the overbuilt Cape Fear & Yadkin Valley Railway was in financial disarray and was subsequently forced into bankruptcy. After four years in receivership, the railroad was still unable to meet its bond obligations. On December 29, 1898, a public sale of the line was held in Fayetteville. Prior to the sale, the bankruptcy judge ordered that the entire line had to remain intact as a single operating unit. At that time, the Wilmington & Weldon Railway (soon to become a part of the Atlantic Coast Railroad) was interested in gaining control of the Bennettsville branch and hoped to do so at a bargain price. Southern Railway, however, was also interested in parts of the line, and a bidding war ensued. The bidding was won by the Wilmington & Weldon Railway, it is said, with the president of Southern Railway's suggestion of a joint ownership account. For a variety of reasons, in 1899 the Wilmington & Weldon Railway chartered a new company, the Atlantic & Yadkin Railroad, to hold the former Cape Fear & Yadkin Valley Railway. A few months later, the entire Atlantic & Yadkin Railroad was sold to the Southern Railway. It immediately chartered a new company, the Atlantic & Yadkin Railway, to hold the line and then sold off the portion from Sanford to Wilmington and from Fayetteville to Bennettsville to the newly named Atlantic Coast Line Railroad. The Atlantic & Yadkin was to be in name only; however, court issues forced the Southern Railway to carve the line back out of its normal operations and revived the legal name of the Atlantic & Yadkin Railway. It created a separate board for the line and placed its headquarters in Greensboro. In 1950, the line was reincorporated back into the Southern Railway.

In the meantime, on August 16, 1894, the lease of the original North Carolina Railroad was assumed by the Southern Railway, which became the single provider of all passenger train services in Greensboro. The path was now opened for the creation of today's J. Douglas Galyon Depot.

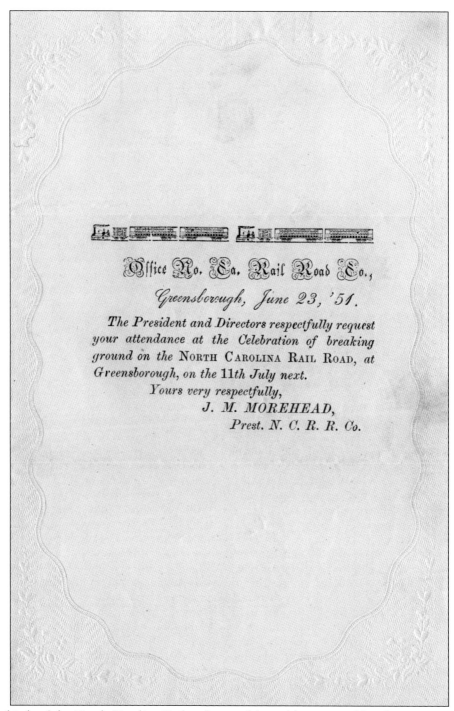

The birth of the North Carolina Railroad was celebrated by a ground-breaking ceremony in downtown Greensboro on July 11, 1851. Former governor John Motley Morehead presided as president of the railroad. Calvin Graves of Caswell County, who had cast the deciding vote in the North Carolina Senate that granted the railroad its charter, turned the first shovel of dirt. (Courtesy of the Greensboro History Museum.)

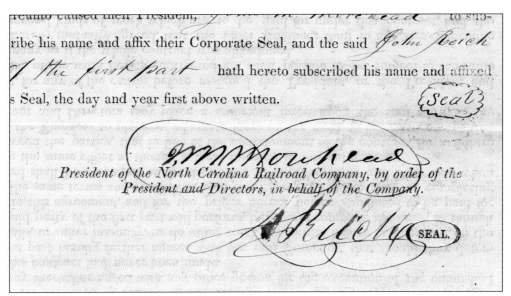

The 1851 signature of Governor Morehead, as president of the North Carolina Railroad (NCRR), is seen here on a contract to build a portion of the railroad. Morehead was instrumental in bringing the NCRR to his home city of Greensboro. His passion for bringing railroads to Greensboro ultimately made the city a railroad hub that garnered it the name Gate City. (Courtesy of the Greensboro History Museum.)

This early undated photograph shows what is believed to have been the first Greensboro passenger depot built by the North Carolina Railroad in 1857. It is often referred to as the Richmond & Danville depot. (Courtesy of the Greensboro History Museum.)

Removed.

Greensboro, N.C. Yard office y-418-2.

Greensboro, N.C. Yard Office.

This 1917 photograph, from Southern Railway's Interstate Commerce Commission (ICC) valuation report, labels the building as the "Greensboro, N.C. Yard Office." By 1867, a wooden depot replaced this as the passenger station and served both the NCRR and the Piedmont Railroad.

Taken from atop the soon-to-be-removed wooden water tank, this photograph faces north looking down at the old North Carolina Railroad depot. During the week of January 28, 1926, Southern Railway used a steam shovel to demolish the building, allowing for the northern entrance to the Davie Street underpass to be built.

This may be the last photograph taken of what is marked as the "office," which was the former North Carolina Railroad depot. This photograph was taken in January 1926, the same month the building was demolished. It was moved at least twice to make room for a bigger wooden depot and tracks. This depot was later used as an office, store shed, eating house, and oil house.

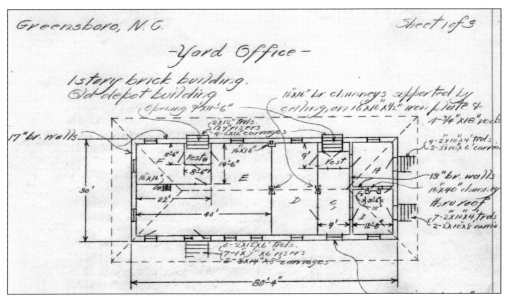

This floor plan of the 1857 depot was drawn in 1916 for the ICC valuation and shows the building as a "Yard Office." The brick walls were 22 inches thick at the base and 17 inches above the interior floor line. The very small waiting room demanded that this depot be replaced by a larger, between-the-tracks version after the Civil War.

There are very few relics left from the North Carolina Railroad. This conductor's uniform cuff button features the typical NC monogram of an interlocked "N" and "C" flanked by the "R" and "R" representing "Rail Road." The button probably dates to the 1870s. (Courtesy of the Greensboro Chapter of the NRHS.)

This is a July 7, 1852, receipt for an installment payment toward eight shares of stock in the North Carolina Railroad. Citizens across North Carolina invested in the railroad, especially those who hoped the line would be constructed along their own property. (Courtesy of the Greensboro History Museum.)

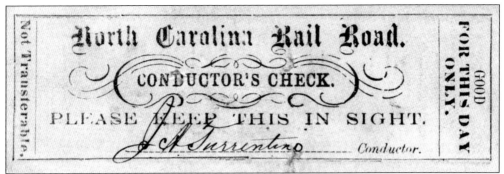

North Carolina Rail Road.

CONDUCTOR'S CHECK.

PLEASE KEEP THIS IN SIGHT.

J. A. Surrentino _____ Conductor.

STATIONS.	Dist.
Charlotte,	0
Harrisburg,	13
Concord,	8
China Grove,	13
Salisbury,	9
Holtsburg,	8
Lexington,	9
Thomasville,	11
High Point,	7
Jamestown,	5
Greensboro',	10
McLean's,	8
Gibsonvil'e,	7
Company Shops,	7
Graham,	2
Haw River,	2
Mebane's,	6
Hillsboro',	10
University Station	5
Durham's,	9
Morrisville,	13
Raleigh,	12
Stallings',	15
Smithfield,	12
Boon Hill,	10
Goldsboro',	12
Total No. Miles,	**223**

This undated ticket for the North Carolina Railroad must predate 1871, when the Richmond & Danville Railroad took over running the line from Goldsboro to Charlotte. The reverse of the ticket lists 26 station stops on the 223-mile line. (Both, courtesy of the Greensboro History Museum.)

This wood-burning American-style 4-4-0 was one of the North Carolina Railroad's engines. The engine number, location, and date are unknown. The NCRR operated as a working railroad until September 1871, when the line was leased by the Richmond & Danville Railroad.

A 4-4-0 American-style engine powered by burning wood is seen outside the engine shops at Company Shops, NC, part of the North Carolina Railroad. The site of Company Shops was later incorporated as Burlington, North Carolina. Some of the original NCRR facilities remain standing.

Mr. Hon. D. W. Kilbourn

Vice Presdt. D. M. V. R. R.

WILL PASS FREE OVER THE

NORTH CAROLINA RAIL ROAD.

During the Year 1867.

Company Shops, N. C.,

Jany 5th, 1867.

Rail passes were used as complimentary passenger tickets across the railroad's system. The above 1867 rail pass for the North Carolina Railroad was issued to David W. Kilbourn, vice president of the Des Moines Valley Railroad, and the below pass was issued to him a couple years later when he was president of the railroad. Passes were good only during the year issued. (Both, courtesy of the Greensboro Chapter of the NRHS.)

PASS BUT ONE PERSON.

NOT TRANSFERABLE.

North Carolina Rail Road,

1869

Pass Hon. D H Kilbourne Esqr

President Des Moines Valley Rail Road

Until December 31, 1869, unless otherwise ordered.

No 167 W. A. Smith Pres't.

The Cape Fear & Yadkin Valley Railway depot is seen from Elm Street as mail from a US mail wagon is loaded between a railway post office car. CF&YV 4-4-0 engine No. 18 was built in 1889 by Baldwin Locomotive Works and subsequently went to the Atlantic & Yadkin (A&Y) and then the Southern. It was scrapped in 1922. (Courtesy of the Greensboro History Museum.)

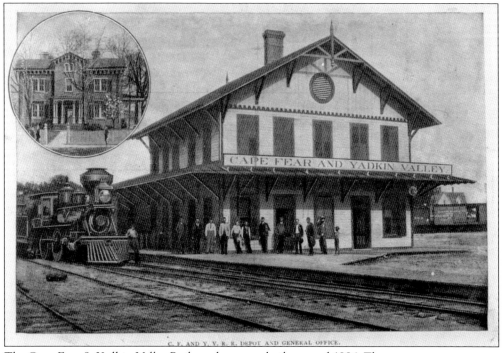

The Cape Fear & Yadkin Valley Railway depot was built around 1884. The two-story structure sat across the tracks from the present home of the 1927 depot. At the time, the Richmond & Danville used a wooden structure wedged between the North Carolina Railroad mainline track and the Piedmont Railroad track. (Courtesy of the Greensboro History Museum.)

Son-in-law of Governor Morehead, Col. Julius Gray was the president of the Cape Fear & Yadkin Railway when it moved its headquarters to Greensboro. In addition to being the founder and first president of the city's chamber of commerce, he also was instrumental in preserving the city's Revolutionary War battlefield. (Courtesy of the Greensboro History Museum.)

Cape Fear & Yadkin Valley Railway (CF&YV) cuff and jacket buttons from a conductor's uniform from about 1886 are pictured here. The CF&YV reached from Wilmington to Mount Airy and was the predecessor road to the Atlantic & Yadkin Railway. (Courtesy of the Greensboro Chapter of the NRHS.)

Cape Fear & Yadkin Valley 4-6-0 engine No. 30 was built in 1896. It was transferred to the Southern Railway as part of the Atlantic & Yadkin and was renumbered to 699 in 1902, then 1413 the next year, and finally 3413. Under the Southern, it was considered an E-class 10-wheeler. She was retired in March 1934.

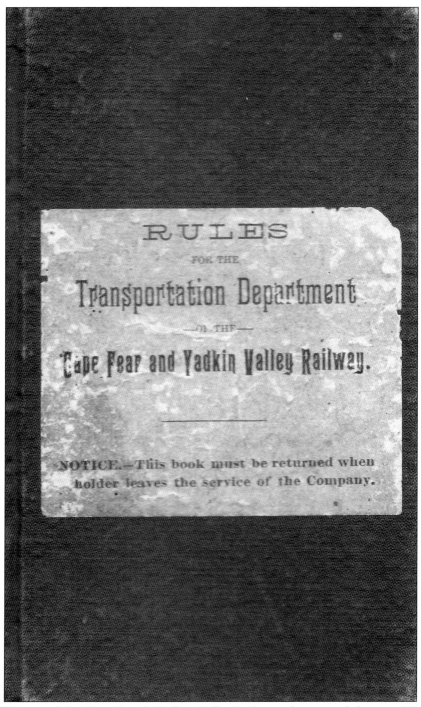

This 1888 copy of the Cape Fear & Yadkin Valley Railway rules covered the use of Standard Time, timetables, and even the use of profanity and unnecessary conversation on the railroad. All railroad employees whose duties were covered in the rule book were required to know all the rules and "must always have a copy of them at hand when on duty." (Courtesy of the Greensboro Chapter of the NRHS.)

The Piedmont Railroad line stretched from Danville to Greensboro and was built at the direction of the Confederate states to aid in transporting war materiel across the border. The line was managed by the Richmond & Danville Railroad—a contention for many North Carolinians. The May 7, 1862, waybill is for 140 sacks of corn. (Courtesy of the Greensboro History Museum.)

This 1880 rail pass for the Richmond & Danville Railroad allowed a person to travel for free on the line. They were usually provided in a reciprocal agreement with other railroads as a professional courtesy. (Courtesy of the Greensboro History Museum.)

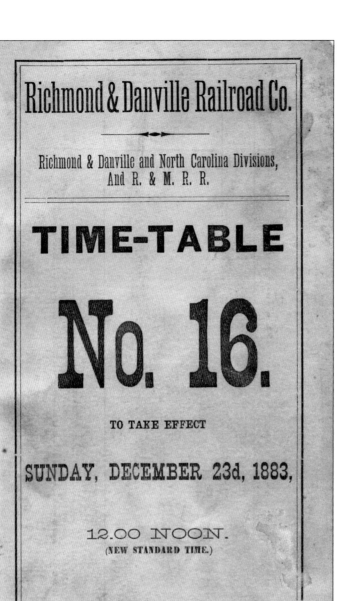

Richmond & Danville Railroad Co.

Richmond & Danville and North Carolina Divisions,
And R. & M. R. R.

TIME-TABLE

No. 16.

TO TAKE EFFECT

SUNDAY, DECEMBER 23d, 1883,

12.00 NOON.
(NEW STANDARD TIME.)

☞ This Time-Table is for the Use of the Employees only,
and not to be considered as information for the public.

Timetables, in conjunction with the train order system, were instrumental in keeping railroads safe at a time before railroad signals and train detection systems were used. Timetables list stations and the departure of various trains due at each location. This December 23, 1883, timetable is from the Richmond & Danville Railroad. (Courtesy of the Greensboro Chapter of the NRHS.)

This is an 1890 first-class ticket to ride from Spartanburg, South Carolina, to Charlotte on the Richmond & Danville Railroad. Like tickets today, this one has restrictions and limits liability to $100 for lost "wearing apparel." (Courtesy of the Greensboro History Museum.)

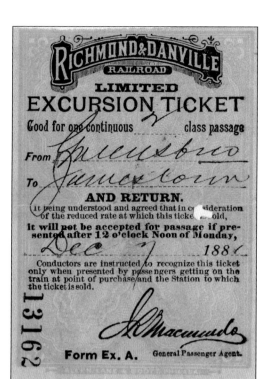

Before the age of television, special events were a main source of entertainment. Political speeches, historic remembrances, and celebrations drove the railroads to offer special train trips to facilitate travel to these events. This 1888 excursion ticket was used for one of those special trips on the Richmond & Danville Railroad, from Greensboro to Jamestown, North Carolina. (Courtesy of the Greensboro History Museum.)

A broadside posted in Greensboro on May 15, 1874, admonishes those riding horseback on the Richmond & Danville roadbed to stop as it was causing damage. The notice warns that riding a horse on the railbed is a misdemeanor crime and also is trespassing. (Courtesy of the Greensboro History Museum.)

NOTICE!

It having been reported at this office that on some sections of the Company's line, especially on the North Carolina Division, parties are in the habit of riding on horse-back on the road-bed.

This, therefore, is to give notice that it is damaging to the road-bed and in violation of the rules, is a **MISDEMEANOR** and **TRESPASS** on the rights and interest of the Company, and subjects the offender to the penalties of the law.

Persons are, therefore, respectfully requested and warned to bear the above in mind and desist, that all trouble may be avoided in the future.

ROGER P. ATKINSON,

Master Roadway and Buildings R. & D. R. R.

Greensboro, N. C., May 15th, 1874.

In January 1896, the Liberty Bell, which was sent to the Atlanta Exposition, stopped in Greensboro on its return trip to Independence Hall. The bell was pulled into the downtown station by the Southern Railway (above) and, after an hour, was transferred to the Cape Fear & Yadkin Valley to continue its journey to the Guilford Courthouse battlefield (below). The local paper estimated that 10,000 people assembled to see the bell. (Both, courtesy of the Greensboro History Museum.)

Atlantic & Yadkin/Southern Railway engine No. 19 is seen on the wye crossing Elm Street in downtown Greensboro in about 1900. The passenger cars sit on the North Carolina Railroad mainline, which was leased by the Southern Railway. The Cascade Saloon is the prominent building on the left, and the 1899 Southern Railway depot is obscured behind it. (Courtesy of the Greensboro History Museum.)

Two

Plans Fall in Place for
a New Passenger Station

By the end of the 19th century, with Southern Railway operating all of Greensboro's passenger train services, it came as no surprise that the existing stations had become inadequate for the number of passenger trains and the increased number of passengers attempting to use the old, cramped facility. Southern undertook the building of a new, spacious station on the north side of the tracks on South Elm Street, which the railroad boasted would serve Greensboro's purposes for the next 50 years. Designed in Richardson Romanesque style, featuring a grand three-story turret, the station had elaborately patterned brickwork and an array of dormer windows topped off with finials and a clay tile roof. The 1899 depot was the pride of the city and the latest word in station facilities for the era.

The 50 years of life, however, that the railroad had envisioned for the station became only ten years, when the citizens of Greensboro began to clamor that the Southern depot was already insufficient for the growing town that could now boast of some 90 daily passenger trains. In 1890, Greensboro's population was only 3,317; by 1905, it had nearly quadrupled. Beginning in 1915, the local press and the chamber of commerce opened the subject for discussion and kept it alive until a new station was completed. Progress languished until 1918, when it stopped with the entry of America into World War I and the federal government's takeover of the railroads. After the war, beginning in 1920, the chamber of commerce, now under the presidency of Jake R. Oettinger, began again to advocate for the building of a new station. Returning for a second time, F. Howie and E.H. Copeman came to Greensboro with a few Southern Railway directors. The railroad put its cards on the table: it was nearly bankrupt, owing to the recent government takeover, precluding any further building at that time. The nearly $1 million felt necessary to build a new station was simply not there. Instead, the City of Greensboro was asked to consider funding the station itself in a loan-type arrangement with the railroad.

On August 23, 1920, in a special session of the state legislature, an act was passed allowing the city to vote for the sale of bonds to undertake the financing of the station. Although a bitter fight was begun by a group of individuals determined to defeat the bond issue, on April 11, 1922, the resolution was passed by a vote of 2,115 to 271. The plan at that time called for the building of a new depot between Elm and Davie Streets, and the understanding was that the city would build an underpass at that site to separate vehicular and foot traffic from the railroad right-of-way.

To be satisfied that the act passed by the state legislature was legitimate, the courts reviewed the matter and found it favorable. Bond attorneys, however, raised some new objections, causing yet another year of delay. This time, however, the delay proved to be to the city's advantage.

With the passing of E.H. Copeman, Southern Railway's operations head, Henry Miller assumed the position. Miller came to Greensboro to see for himself what was being contemplated. In his opinion, he determined that the Elm-Davie site was totally inadequate for the kind of station needed at such an important Southern Railway transfer point. The Southern Railway had changed since the devastating years after World War I, and it was on its way to a remarkable recovery. Rather than build an inadequate facility, Miller proposed to cancel the agreement that the city and railroad had negotiated regarding the loan issue. Additionally, he proposed that Southern Railway itself would underwrite the construction of the new station, changing the site to a much larger one located on Washington Street opposite the opening of Forbis Street. He further announced that the railroad would build the necessary underpass at the original Elm-Davie site, even though the Southern was not going to build the station there as originally proposed. Instead, Miller only asked the city to underwrite the construction of an underpass on East Washington Street where a grade crossing at that point was no longer practical. The city had a bargain, and with its acceptance by city fathers, construction of Greensboro's new station could commence at any time.

This undated photograph of the 1899 Southern depot on Elm Street also shows the still-standing Cascade Saloon. Key citizens of the greater Greensboro community joined together to lobby the Southern Railway to build a depot that could accommodate the growing population. When built, the station was self-sufficient in providing its own heat and electricity.

At mile marker 284.1 on the mainline through Greensboro, this is a view of Elm Street looking north—not west as the photograph notes. The 1899 depot can be seen to the left along with a variety of electric street cars, horse-drawn buggies, and automobiles. The high volume of traffic on Elm Street would prompt the Southern Railway to build an underpass with the new 1927 depot to help alleviate traffic delays at this grade crossing.

This panoramic photograph from 1905 shows the main intersection of the railroad and Elm Street, 50 years after trains started traveling along the NCRR mainline. Near the center is the 1899 depot, flanked by the Cascade Saloon to the left and the Clegg Hotel to the right. The roof of the 1857 depot can be seen across the street, behind a string of boxcars. Up and down Elm Street, the city's

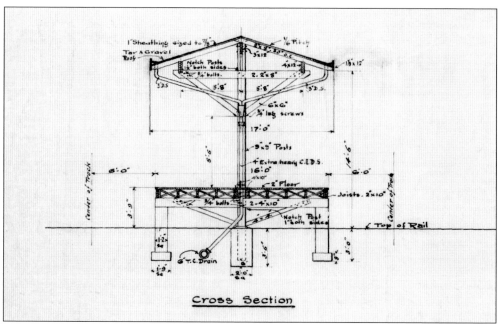

Cross Section

This 1905 plan shows the cross-section of the new freight platforms added to the old Cape Fear & Yadkin Valley depot. With the opening of the 1899 "union" depot on Elm Street, the Southern Railway expanded and repurposed its subsidiary's passenger station into a freight house.

growth is reflected in the multi-story shops lining the main downtown street. At bottom center, a streetcar can be seen heading southbound while an engine travels up the A&Y wye. Greensboro was already starting to boom, and the new, self-sufficient station would soon be overwhelmed by the number of passengers. (Courtesy of the Greensboro History Museum.)

This undated photograph shows one set of the freight platforms illustrated in the plan on the previous page in place. A drawbridge connected this platform to the second one.

On September 17, 1906, crowds of people gather around the tracks on Elm Street to hear a "whistle stop" speech from presidential candidate William Jennings Bryan. Charles Duncan McIver, president of what is now the University of North Carolina Greensboro and friend of Bryan, had died on the train between Durham and Greensboro. Bryan delivered a eulogy for McIver instead. (Courtesy of the Greensboro History Museum.)

Soldiers waiting on the Greensboro Depot passenger platform are greeted by American Red Cross workers. Greensboro was granted a Red Cross chapter in April 1917. Internal Southern Railway documents show the company knew it would have to build a larger station to accommodate the growing passenger business, but the war suspended those plans. (Courtesy of the Greensboro History Museum.)

This 1925 view of 501 Ashe Street—J.R. Pitts Building Materials—in downtown Greensboro shows a train blocking the grade crossing. At this time, Ashe Street crossed the Atlantic & Yadkin wye and the mainline of the Southern Railway. The engine appears to be No. 548, a 2-8-0 class J consolidation that was sometimes rented to the A&Y by the Southern Railway. (Courtesy of the Greensboro History Museum.)

The heavy traffic on Elm Street, and most other downtown streets, was in constant conflict with the railroad grade crossing. Ultimately, a combination of public dissatisfaction coupled with increasing lawsuits from accidents forced the railroad to build underpasses. (Courtesy of the Greensboro History Museum.)

An ad touting the new grade crossing signals on Elm Street almost seems unnecessary with the adjoining Davie Street underpass, but even today, problems persist at this busy crossing. The Southern Railway No. 2902 is an EMD E-6A passenger engine. It is seen crossing Elm Street heading for the 1927 depot. Farther north down Elm Street, the tall Jefferson Standard buildings can be seen.

Looking west along the mainline, cars, buses, and streetcars all traverse the railroad. This photograph appears to be from the early 1920s and again highlights the amount of traffic crossing the busy railroad. The 1899 depot (center) and the 1857 depot (right) dominate the scene.

This postcard of the 1899 depot in Greensboro was postmarked in 1907. It shows the two passenger shelters, with one integral to the building and a second between the tracks. Water was provided to the steam engines by way of a standpipe fed by one of two aboveground water tanks near Elm Street. The water tanks were removed during the construction of the new depot and replaced by a single big metal tank. (Courtesy of the Greensboro Chapter of the NRHS.)

Julius Cone along with Elaine Cone and Sophie Wolf are seen outside the 1899 depot on Elm Street sometime around 1908. Behind the car is the 1857 depot. Julius Cone along with his brothers Moses and Caesar and his father, Herman, owned Cone Export & Commission Company and later Cone Mills, which manufactured denim in Greensboro. (Courtesy of the Greensboro History Museum.)

One of many US presidents to visit Greensboro, former president Theodore "Teddy" Roosevelt gives a speech on October 1, 1912, as he wraps up a whistle-stop tour of the South. Just a couple of weeks later, he was shot while campaigning in Milwaukee, Wisconsin. (Courtesy of the Greensboro History Museum.)

Southern Railway dispatchers stand in one of the doorways of the old 1857 depot. Prior to the building of the 1927 depot, the railroad employees worked in a variety of locations across the city. When the new depot was finally built, the railroad closed its satellite offices and consolidated them in the 1899 depot. (Courtesy of the Greensboro History Museum.)

A wrecked car sits on the tracks in downtown Greensboro. Accidents like this were happening frequently and caused a lot of anxiety within the community. Ultimately, the concerns for safety led to the building of underpasses in and around downtown. Both the Washington Street and Davie Street underpasses were added to the agreement with the city during negotiations for funding for the depot project. Both photographs are of the same accident. (Above, courtesy of the Greensboro History Museum; below, courtesy of the Bernie Simmons Collection, the Greensboro Chapter of the NRHS.)

The 1899 depot was photographed as part of the railroad's ICC filings in 1916, and while it was only 15 years old at the time, it was already not big enough to accommodate the area's traffic. The below August 7, 1920, internal Southern Railway memo highlights the problem the railroad already had with its relatively new downtown depot. Greensboro's train station was the busiest on the line, and the facility could not meet the demands of the growing population.

Uptown City Ticket Office - Greensboro, N. C.

Washington - August 7, 1920 - hel

MR. HARRISON;

     Please approve.

     We formerly maintained an uptown ticket office at Greensboro, but tried to avoid it in the new organization. This is one of the heaviest passenger stations on the System and we cannot handle the situation satisfactorily at the present expense. The Chamber of Commerce at Greensboro is complaining about the lack of service and I believe the demand for an uptown office a very reasonable one.

           L. G.

L. G.

Agreed if it is understood that this is a temporary relief until a new station is built

H Aug 9

Three

CONSTRUCTION COMMENCES

Beginning in January 1926, foundation and track work was underway on the East Washington Street station site. On the morning of Wednesday, March 10, 1926, Gus Ginn, a Gastonia, North Carolina, contractor, using the steam shovel of the Nello Teer Company, which owned the Durham & Southern Railway, was given the contract for the grading of the station grounds, although Consolidated Engineering was scheduled to do the actual excavation of the 12,000 cubic yards of dirt. Wintry weather hindered the operation for a few days, but on March 16, the steam shovel and related wagons were reported busy at work once again. On March 8, a large group of laborers had started excavation for the building's footing. A considerable amount of dirt was reported to have already been moved at the station site.

In addition to the work that was underway at the station itself, work was also in progress on the Washington Street and Elm-Davie underpasses. At the latter, the old Southern Railway mainline tracks had already been torn away and new ones positioned. Much of the concrete on one side of the Washington Street underpass had already been poured. By March 27, 1926, Consolidated Engineering Company already had a traveling crane on site ready to pour the station's concrete foundation and erect the steel as soon as the ground was prepared. Initial work on the main station building itself commenced on April 14, while footings on the station building were poured beginning April 21.

On Friday, April 23, 1926, two-thirds of the foundation work on the new subway being built beneath the station tracks had been completed to the point that beginning that morning, work started on pouring the concrete for the side walls of the subway under the tracks overhead. The remaining third could not be laid until the tracks had been shifted into their new positions. Sub-contracts had already been secured for the station's steelwork to be done by Virginia Bridge & Iron Company, the heating contract had been awarded to R. MacKenzie of Greensboro, the lumber contract to the local firm of Oettinger Lumber Company, and the plumbing contract was awarded to Toomey Brothers of Charlotte.

May 2 brought the announcement that the station building's concrete foundations were rapidly being completed and forms for pouring concrete around part of the station itself were being built, heavily reinforced with steel bars. Some piles were also being driven in the subway area beneath the tracks.

By May 5, total excavation had been accomplished, and tons of concrete were being poured daily. Simultaneously, the Northeastern Construction Company was completing its work on the East Washington Street underpass. The walls and concrete bases for the underpass had already been poured, but the steel beams and supports remained to be completed. In a short time, plans called for the company to move its equipment to the Elm-Davie underpass site where Southern Railway's tracks had already been detoured and sufficient excavation had been accomplished to warrant the commencement of actual work.

On the morning of Wednesday, March 10, 1926, Gus Ginnusing used a steam shovel of the Nello Teer Company (which owned the Durham & Southern Railway)—like the one pictured—to start the grading of the station grounds. To the left is a truck manufactured in Cadillac, Michigan, by the Acme Motor Truck Company. Acme stopped making trucks in 1929.

Soon after starting the excavations, a large amount of dirt was removed by steam shovels and many laborers. Interestingly, this excavator is a gas-powered shovel manufactured by the Osgood Shovel Company of Marion, Ohio. It is marked "1¼ YD Heavy Duty." The company flourished from 1912 until 1954.

Work is underway on the Washington Street and Davie Street underpasses. Southern Railway's steam-powered pile driver PD-24 drives temporary piles to support the mainline. The railroad owned a handful of pile drivers, and this one was built in 1912 by Industrial Works of Bay City, Michigan.

Piles have been driven along the mainline, and even in between the rails, to temporarily shore up the tracks so the construction crews can remove the earth below. The crews will build a trestle at ground level so the existing track bridges the new road being built underneath the railroad. The wooden piles will be immediately replaced with a steel and concrete structure.

A steam Southern Railway pile driver works along the mainline in Greensboro. As part of the new depot construction in 1926, the railroad lowered both Washington and Davie Streets in downtown Greensboro. Piles were driven into the railroad roadbed to provide track support while the street was excavated below, ultimately replaced by a steel bridge.

The work shoring up the mainlines with piles has already taken place, and the old 1857 North Carolina Railroad depot has been razed. A steam shovel works in the background excavating the area that will be the Davie Street underpass. Note that while there is one open-cab dump truck, the bulk of the earth is being carted off in wagons.

In 1926, manpower was inexpensive. Large crews of laborers worked hard to dig the depot's foundation by hand. As the crews dug, they used lumber to brace their trenches that would later be filled with poured concrete. In the background, a heavy steel hoist, which was installed on March 27, 1926, is ready to aid in the pouring of the station's concrete foundation and the erection of the steel.

Piles and a temporary trestle have been installed on the mainline just east of Elm Street. Soon, the new Davie Street underpass will be in place and traffic will be able to safely travel under the Southern Railway mainline. This and the Washington Street underpass projects were included as part of the depot building project. Within a few years, other underpass projects would spring up around town.

Excavation of Washington Street, with the depot area to the right, progresses with a steam shovel seen in front of the Whitman-Douglas Company—a provider of wholesale heating and plumbing supplies. The company occupied 325–327 East Washington Street. Beyond the building, the Washington Street underpass will soon be built.

Concrete pipes are being unloaded for the drainage of reconstructed downtown roads, needed to ensure free-flowing traffic as Southern Railway builds its new depot. The building of the new station changed the automotive traffic flow significantly in downtown Greensboro, untethering the traffic patterns from delays caused by the railroad. Essentially, those changes remain today.

Southern Railway camp cars line the siding as construction crews install ballast deck girder bridges over Washington Street on the east side of the depot construction project. Like Davie Street, Washington Street was excavated below the railroad grade. These bridges are being installed on the former Piedmont Air Line, which runs from the depot to Danville, Virginia, and beyond.

Ties and trestle timbers are stacked just north of the mainline as work continues to get ready for the excavation under Davie Street. The steam-powered pile driver can be seen in the background along with the former Cape Fear & Yadkin Valley depot; expanded into the Southern Railway freight depot, it became the Atlantic & Yadkin Railway and was purchased by the Southern Railway.

The tracks leading to the Southern Railway freight house, opposite the building site for the new depot, have been removed as the Davie Street underpass work proceeds. The freight house would continue to be used as a transfer warehouse for decades. The small yard that surrounded the old structure is still used today and is referred to as the A&Y Yard.

This view is from what will be the interior of the depot, looking south toward the mainlines. The foundation walls are visible, as is the steel structure that will brace the tunnel to the three platforms. Originally, a single tunnel served the platforms. With the remodel in 2001, a separate tunnel was constructed to handle baggage and other non-passenger traffic.

Looking west on Washington Street, the deck girder bridge construction is well underway. In the foreground is the shoo-fly (bypass) track that kept the line open to Danville. The former Piedmont Air Line was built by the Confederate States of America during the Civil War, overcoming a long-standing reluctance to connect the North Carolina Railroad with Virginia. The building in the background still stands today.

Several buildings had to be razed to make room for the new depot and associated construction. In the background is a billboard for the Cook-Lewis Foundry, located on the Southern Railway line at Fulton Street. Visible just above the interesting, junked truck is what appears to be the remnants of a press.

Southern Railway camp cars sit isolated on an incomplete track that is being laid to accommodate the Washington Street underpass. Camp cars were used to house work crews and included barracks cars, kitchens, and tool shops on the work site.

Drainage pipes lay at the ready as a guyed derrick equipped with a pile driver stands near the excavation for the Davie Street underpass. In the background are the Cascade Saloon and the 1899 depot. The Cascade Saloon was erected in 1895 and still stands today, thanks to a monumental effort to save and renovate this historic building.

Here is another view of the guyed derrick with the pole driver apparatus attached. The placed piles are surrounded by wooden cribbing that will be used to cast in place the concrete retaining walls for the Davie Street underpass. In the background are a maintenance-of-way coach and a string of ventilated boxcars.

Construction is moving rapidly on the Davie Street underpass. Bridge girders are being assembled for the underpass with a guyed derrick sitting among piles to be driven to reinforce the bridge construction. A watchman sits on a fence next to his new shanty, a temporary replacement for the one removed for construction.

A vertical boiler engine and the guyed derrick sit in the middle of piles of bridge deck girders (steel beams) as work continues on the Davie Street underpass. The string of railroad passenger cars highlights the need to allow traffic to travel through downtown Greensboro, especially with the anticipated passenger traffic the new station was being built to handle.

A tractor pulls a wagon used in the grading process. During the construction of the depot and associated projects, there was an interesting blend of manual labor, steam power, and even combustion engines.

In the age of steam, even the construction equipment was powered by burning coal. Here, an Erie steam shovel is finishing up work lowering one of the many streets so that automobile traffic can easily pass under the Southern Railway's mainline. The cost of lowering these roads was deemed necessary based on the danger caused by automobiles crossing railroad tracks.

Four

STATION CONSTRUCTION
INTENSIFIES

May 17, 1926, brought the welcome news that two carloads of structural steel had been unloaded by the Virginia Bridge & Iron Company and were to be used in the subway being built just behind the station leading to the tracks overhead. By May 28, the first steel was being positioned. By May 30, all the concrete work for the subway that could be completed had been readied, as well as the concrete foundations for the station. In a few days, work could begin on the construction of the actual station walls. On that same date, the overhead steel structure for the subway section of the station was almost finished. In conjunction with the work on storm sewers being readied for the building of the two Washington Street and the Elm-Davie underpasses, the east end of Southern Railway's old freight depot, discarded some years before, was being cleared. This was followed beginning July 6 by the razing of the west end of the old freight station to allow for the construction of the Elm-Davie underpass. A large work crew was busy riveting steel, and another was completing the forms for the concrete gangway. Southern Railway crews were grading for the tracks leading into the new station so that all could be ready for the switching to permanent mainline tracks as soon as the portion of the underpass under the mainline was completed. Work would then commence on the south side of the mainline opening to South Elm and Fayetteville Streets.

Station superintendent D.H. Hutchins reported on July 13 that the entire steel framing for the station would be erected and riveted by July 22 and the stone and brick work would commence July 16. He estimated prematurely that at the pace work was progressing, the station could be opened before the specified time of March 1927. Tracks were being laid over the Washington Street underpass.

On July 19, 1926, the local media reported that the steel framework for the central roof of the station was being positioned and a large force of workmen was rapidly riveting the steel together. Two tracks were already laid on the bridge crossing the Washington Street underpass in two sections. The work of laying the rails across the new route via the station was pushed, and it was hoped that in a few days, work could be finalized. A large portion of track was placed between the new station and Davie Street in readiness for cutting it in as soon as the Davie-Elm underpass concrete work could be completed.

On August 6, Stewart Wagner with the architectural firm of Fellheimer & Wagner, designers of the building, was in town with two Consolidated Engineering Company engineers and met with Mayor E.B. Jeffress. All appeared pleased with the progress that had been made on the new station. The promise then was that the station building would be ready for use on January 1, 1927. The entire station's steel work was already in place and masonry work was getting underway. On August 13, Southern Railway vice president Henry W. Miller arrived in town aboard train No. 34. He reiterated the comments of the others involved in the station's construction, who on August 6 had remarked on their satisfaction with the work. To iron out details in the construction, on the night of August 18, 1926, Greensboro mayor Jeffress left for Washington, DC, to confer with Southern Railway vice president Miller.

On August 27, Southern Railway workmen removed the watchman's tower at the South Elm crossing, temporarily placing the watchman in a shanty until the watchman's job there would no longer be necessary. Removal of the tower was necessitated by the need to shift the tracks of Southern

Railway's subsidiary the Atlantic & Yadkin Railway across South Elm farther to the north so they could be connected to Southern's mainline when the tracks were laid over the underpass and the existing line could be torn out to permit excavation for the south end of the underpass. At that time, a second coating of concrete was applied to the southbound track over the underpass, and track had already been laid directly up to that point. As soon as the concrete sufficiently cured, the work of putting in the crossties and rails was pushed, and connection could then be made into the present line in front of the station. The southbound traffic could then be shifted to that track, and the old line could be torn out. A few days later, the northbound track was shifted as well. The change in the A&Y track across South Elm was to bring the track several feet farther north than at present and eliminate the unwanted curve at the far end of the crossing.

On September 3, 1926, the papers reported that although the station was not ready for actual occupancy, around September 15, the first train would begin to use the new mainline route that would take it by the new station. This was made possible by the fact that the rails over the bridges at East Washington Street and between South Elm and South Davie would be ready for use. On September 14, Southern Railway train No. 154 became the first passenger train to pass by the still-incomplete station.

On October 17, 1926, the walls of the main station building were about complete, and the rough concrete floor foundations had been poured. Excavation for the more distant tracks at the station was nearing completion and the foundation for the separate express building was underway. The mail and baggage rooms were also rapidly taking shape, and it was thought that within a short time, the roof could be placed over that wing of the station.

Above, the excavation of the Davie Street underpass has progressed, uncovering a portion of the wooden piles used to facilitate the continued use of the track before the steel bridges were built. A steam-powered derrick sits on top of the excavation. Below, a Southern Railway yard engine, No. 1684, an A-7 class 0-6-0 switcher, is shunting a Reading Railroad gondola on a near track supported by the temporary piles set for the underpass excavation. No. 1684 was shared between the Southern and the Atlantic & Yadkin Railways.

Work is well underway in this May 30, 1926, photograph of the depot construction site. The foreground tracks are temporary shoo-fly tracks that allowed for the construction of the passenger tunnel under the mainlines. In the background is a building advertising Watson Feed Company, which would later become Wafco Mills when it moved a few blocks west.

By May's end, the concrete and steel work was completed for the passenger tunnels to the platforms. Contemporary sources sometimes referred to the tunnels as subways. The girder bridge style supports for the mainline would be buried out of sight until the later replacement that was part of the depot's 2001 renovations. The Jefferson Standard building is in the background.

This interesting piece of equipment is half-tracked, and appears to be working on one of the many excavations in and around the construction site—maybe the passenger tunnels. While the exact purpose of the machine is unknown, it is likely a concrete mixer.

The foundation of the depot is under construction. Completed in 1923, the Jefferson Standard building is in the background. When this photograph was taken, Julian Price was president of both Jefferson Standard Life Insurance and the Atlantic & Yadkin Railway, a subsidiary of the Southern Railway

Station superintendent D.H. Hutchins reported on July 13, 1926, that the entire steel framing for the station would be erected and riveted by July 22, when the stone and brickwork would commence. He estimated (incorrectly) that at this pace, the station could be opened before the specified time of March 1927.

Another of Southern Railway's steam-powered pile drivers, PD-19, is seen working to support the underpass construction for the mainline through Greensboro. The excavation of various street underpasses near the depot necessitated the installation of temporary pile-driven trestles. The railroad owned a handful of pile drivers, and this one was built sometime between 1904 and 1908.

The brick façade of the depot starts to take shape and the steel structure provides an outline of what will come. On October 17, 1926, it was reported that the walls of the main station building were about complete, and the rough concrete floor foundations had been poured.

An unloaded Southern Railway boxcar is seen somewhere near the construction site. This boxcar, No. 157680, was built between 1922 and 1923. Known by the Southern as an SU-class boxcar, these 36-foot-long, truss-rod cars seemed like a throwback for a time that saw the building of much more modern rolling stock.

A steam pile driver is working in the area soon to be the Davie Street underpass. The former Cape Fear & Yadkin Valley depot is on the right.

Work is progressing on the Washington Street underpass. Behind the bridge are three Southern Railway camp cars, with another three off to the right. Behind the camp cars is the Sergeant Manufacturing Company building, which still stands today.

Here is another view of the Washington Street underpass being built. To the right, the steel frame being erected on the depot can be seen. The tracks to the left are temporary shoo-fly tracks that allow trains to continue to run north toward Danville while the underpass is under construction.

A couple of stationary steam engines sit in the staging yard by the guyed derrick. The large freight house fills the photograph, and the Jefferson Standard building is in the background.

Looking west toward the old 1899 Southern Railway depot, an Erie steam shovel starts working as mule carts and trucks patiently wait nearby. The soon-to-be-replaced wooden water tower can be seen to the left, as well as a steam locomotive that finds itself slipping between work cars and coaches.

Here is a close-up shot of the pile driver's hammer in operation. The view is looking northeast, with the Greensboro Supply building in the background. The depot will be built just to the right.

Greensboro's skyline was almost solely defined by one of the tallest buildings in the South, the Jefferson Standard building. In the foreground is the freight house and the old "yard office," which was the former North Carolina Railroad depot.

With the wooden water tower to the left and the 1899 Southern Railway depot to the right, the African American–owned Cascade Saloon is seen at center. In this photograph, the facade reads "Central Cafe." In the foreground are various construction carts and a small concrete mixer.

A Southern Railway open platform wooden day coach in maintenance service is seen near the excavations of the passenger tunnel that will access the platforms. Like many railroads, the Southern Railway utilized obsolete coaches as parts of work trains. They were refitted to serve a variety of purposes, including bunk cars, tool cars, and even classrooms.

The steel supports for the passenger canopies are being erected for the passenger platforms, which are still to be poured. To the left, the depot construction has also started.

The new steel water tower is in place, as are the new passenger platforms. A water crane (standpipe) can be seen on the end of the mainline platform. Water cranes were used to deliver water to the steam locomotive's tender and were more convenient than building large water towers adjacent to the tracks.

Rough-hewn logs sit in the foreground waiting their turn to be installed as the pile driver prepares the track for excavation that will allow for the needed underpasses around Greensboro.

The Erie steam shovel operator can be clearly seen manipulating the "sea of levers" used to operate this modern marvel of excavation. Various camp cars and coaches can be seen in the background, all painted in the light colors of a work train.

This nice side view of a Southern Railway pile driver shows the steam-powered driver and the associated tender needed to keep the unit running. The photograph appears to show that the railroad married an old tender to a larger flat car and added some sort of tool shed.

Laborers sit on a small push car on the new Washington Street underpass. Nine camp cars can be seen in the background, along with a variety of other maintenance cars, a steam shovel, and the old Cape Fear & Yadkin Valley depot.

Above, this side view of the construction of the depot was taken August 26, 1926. The steel arches are in place for the large, curved windows of the main concourse. Washington Street is to the right. The construction is a steel structure with a brick and stone façade. Taken at the same time, the below track-side view shows how rapidly the construction proceeded. The gap in the mainline track is above the tunnel between the station and the platforms.

Five

CONSTRUCTION
NEARS COMPLETION

On October 12, 1926, work of pouring the concrete floors for the waiting rooms and offices on the first floor was near completion. The walls of the main building were similarly nearing completion, except for the parapet top. Walls of the mail and baggage rooms in the right wing from the central passageway were going up, and construction of the express building was also underway. Steam shovels were busy doing grading work for the third line of mainline tracks and excavation for the extension of the underpass there. Railroad officials admitted, however, for the first time that there still remained "a great deal of work" to be completed if the station was to meet its projected April 1, 1927, opening date.

The November 7, 1926, paper reported splendid progress on the station. With a few more weeks of favorable weather, it was promised that the entire outside construction would be completed and considerable interior detail work would be accomplished as well. Work of pouring the roof over the central part of the building was nearing completion. The large columns in front of the station had already been positioned, with the exception of the huge space that would extend from one column to the other and connect the columns with the building. The walls for the mail transfer quarters and the baggage room were about ready for the placing of the roof, while the concrete foundations for the offices and rooms of the Southeastern Express Company had also been positioned. Wide sheds were to be built along the sides of the buildings, making it possible to load and unload baggage, express, and mail without damage from the elements. While workmen were busy on the outside, others were busy on the partitions in the station proper. By this date, all the concrete work on the main station had been completed, as had the conduits for heating, lighting, and the like. Similarly, all the forms for concrete had been built for the extension of the walls of the subway beneath the tracks to beyond the third series of tracks, meaning Track 5 and Track 6, which would allow for the pouring of concrete for the subway roof. Concrete headers around the platforms between the tracks had also been poured, followed by grading and pouring of the platforms themselves. Swinging water pipes for filling the steam locomotive tenders had already been positioned at either end of the platforms. Riveters were busy completing the sealing of the hot bolts in the steelwork of the third span over the Davie underpass, and another crew was completing the backfill in the space from the Atlantic & Yadkin Railway track alongside the west wall of the south approach to the underpass. O.S. Payrant, the engineer for the Fellheimer & Wagner architectural firm building the station, who had designed the plans for the two underpasses, was in town on December 9 in conference with Mayor Jeffress and city manager P.C. Painter.

On page 13 of the December 12, 1926, *Greensboro Record*, there appeared an image of the new station. It depicted the building with exterior work about completed and showed the baggage room and mail room sections to the right of the main station, on the second floor of the main building. Out of frame was the express building, incomplete at that time. For the first time, the paper mentioned that the station would house a drugstore, a barbershop, and numerous railroad offices.

December 18, 1926, was a cold day in Greensboro, well below freezing. Concrete for the walkways under the new steel shelters needed from 16 to 24 hours to set with no freezing. To ensure that they were not ruined, some 100 kerosene smudge pots were brought in and saved the day. By that date, the longest of the three concrete passenger platforms was reported some three-fourths completed, while some of the work for the second one was underway.

January 6, 1927, brought mention by the newspapers that the new station would be open in early spring. Work on the last unit of the station was then well underway. Structural and concrete work on the station proper and the underground passageways were in the process of being completed. Work was also underway on the Southeastern Railway Express building.

The January 23, 1927, paper reported that practically all of the partition walls were in place in the station and quite a bit of the overhead framework for holding the plaster had been placed. With the completion of the plastering and the painting, the next thing on the agenda would be the paving of the composition floors followed by the installation of the fixtures, heating, plumbing, and electrical work, and the furniture itself. The steam plant for the building's heating had been completed and test fires had already been made. On the outside, the work of putting on the tar and gravel roofing on top of stone slabs and roofing paper was going forward rapidly. Another workforce was busy putting the finishing touches to the baggage and mail rooms.

There still remained a considerable amount of platform work about the station. The main passenger platform extending from near Washington Street to the old Davie crossing had been completed as well as much of the second platform. The butterfly sheds that had been erected over the platforms were being treated to a second coat of paint, a dull gray over the initial coat of red. Yet another group of workmen was busy building the entrances to stairways from the subway area to the tracks above. The grading had been accomplished so that tracks could be placed immediately. Grading had by then also been completed for the street and parking space along the rear of the express building and the mail and baggage rooms of the station itself. This extended out to Washington Street. Rough grading had been accomplished for the paving of the driveway space near the main station entrances extending back to Washington Street. Sidewalks had already been completed around the entire circle. Remaining to be done was some exterior work, including the placing of the doors.

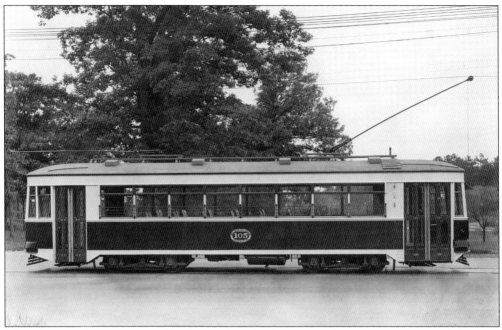

With the new depot to open, North Carolina Public Service Company, operators of the local streetcar and transit system, announced that it would extend its tracks to provide streetcar service directly to the station. At a cost of about $8,000, plans called for the extension of tracks from East Market Street along Forbis Avenue about 800 feet to Washington Street. (Bernie Simmons Collection, the Greensboro Chapter of the NRHS.)

This is a Southern Railway pushcart with a hand brake. These types of track vehicles were found with maintenance-of-way crews all over the system. They were used to transport men and material along the tracks but were light enough to be lifted off the tracks by a couple of workers.

The concrete has been poured and the steelwork is in place as work on the foundation of the depot's passenger tunnel is underway.

Brick, granite, and steel rise on the site of the new station. As expected, the materials for the construction projects were delivered by rail. Interestingly, goods were shipped from all over the country, and cars from a wide variety of railroads could be seen in Greensboro during construction. This Norfolk Southern boxcar was from a small railroad that operated mostly along the coast of North Carolina and Virginia.

On January 28, 1927, Stewart Wagner of the Fellheimer & Wagner architectural firm was back in town, and promised that on or about April 17, the new station would be open for business. By February 20, the entire depot complex was under a completed roof. Looking from the top of the Southeastern Express Company building, even as it snows, work continues at the depot.

Looking from the roof of the station toward the express building, the two skylights can be clearly seen. This photograph dates from October 1962, and the building is occupied by the Railway Express Agency, a successor to the Southeastern Express Company.

It is evident from this photograph that Greensboro was a very busy location along the Southern Railway line. Passenger cars are already occupying space around the passenger platforms while the sheds are being built. (Edward J. McCauley Photographic Materials [P0082], North Carolina Collection Photographic Archives, the Wilson Library, University of North Carolina at Chapel Hill.)

Progress on the Elm Street grade crossing can be seen with the new automatic grade crossing gate and flashing lights installed in front of the soon-to-be-removed pneumatic gates and watch tower. Traffic congestion and an acknowledgment by Southern Railway that this crossing was dangerous prompted the nearby Davie Street underpass to be built.

This undated photograph shows construction underway on the front façade. Pictured is a vertical boiler to the left, a small concrete mixer, an early pickup truck, a two-door coupe (marked "Mulkey's Iodie Salt"), a large work truck, a touring car, and some horses. (Edward J. McCauley Photographic Materials (P0082), North Carolina Collection Photographic Archives, the Wilson Library, University of North Carolina at Chapel Hill.)

In this side view of the depot, it looks like the exterior is close to complete. The parking lot still needs to be paved. This photograph is undated but is marked "received May 5, 1927" by the resident engineer's office in Greensboro. The depot officially opened on April 20.

SOME OBJECTIONS TO THE STATION BONDS

1. While all of us want Greensboro to have a suitable passenger station, the law requires the Railway Company to build this at its own expense.

2. There has never been an organized effort to compel the Railway Company to obey this law by an application to the Corporation Commission.

3. The contention made in behalf of the Railway Company that if the Commission were to make such an order it would not be complied with by the Railway Company should be condemned by all law-abiding citizens.

4. The City is not now in such a financial condition to justify it in borrowing $1,300,000 to loan to the Southern Railway to build the proposed passenger station; our tax rate is already so high that it is oppressive to most of us; the proposed bonds will impair our credit and render it more difficult and expensive for the City to borrow more money, which it seems it will shortly become necessary to do for water works, street improvement and other purposes.

5. The Southern Railway admits that it is so hard pressed for money that it is not able to finance this proposition itself. Its property is mortgaged for $120,000,000.00 and then some; its bonds secured by mortgage sell for around 89; its preferred stock for about 50; and its common stock for about 20. This shows its financial condition.

6. It gives the City no adequate security. It proposes to convey to a Trustee for the City only the land on which the station is erected. This is neither a mortgage nor a deed of trust. It makes the City virtually the owner of the building, which is useless for any City purposes. It contains no provision for a foreclosure, which all mortgages and deeds of trust do, and no such provision can be added to this deed except by consent of the Southern Railway.

7. The Southern Railway says it will pay for the use and occupation of the building and accessories, monthly, a rental sufficient to pay interest on the bonds and to create an adequate sinking fund. It promises to pay this rent only so long as it occupies this building. There is nothing in the Act of the Legislature requiring it to occupy the building any longer than it suits it to do so. The fact that it agrees to pay this rent to the City shows that the City is to be considered the landlord and owner of the property.

8. If the City is the landlord and owner of the property as shown above, and declared in the act, how can the City levy tax against this property any more than it can against the City Hall? It will be tax free.

9. The Act of the Legislature contains the only contract which is binding on the Southern Railway and the City. Nothing can be added to it for the City's protection, except by consent of the Southern Railway Company.

10. An experienced contractor of this City says that it will take at least two years to complete these improvements. Meantime in two years $156,000.00 interest will accrue on the bonds, besides what would have to be paid in order to create a sinking fund. The Southern nowhere promises to pay this, consequently, the City will have to pay it. The Southern promises to pay nothing except rent to commence after the completion of the building.

11. It is not wise for us to vote on ourselves this large bond issue, and then depend on securing from the Southern Railway Company afterward a more favorable contract, which contract it may withhold at its pleasure.

12. The title to the property ought to be ascertained to be good before we are called upon to vote the bonds. We are asked to obligate ourselves and then to litigate all questions afterwards. This would be a very unwise course to pursue.

13. If we are to issue bonds and build a station and rent it to the Southern Railway Company, as provided in the Legislative Act, why should we deed it to the Southern Railway Company at all, why not keep it and continue to rent it?

14. Six per cent. return on an investment is certainly a moderate rental; if so, this would pay for the property in sixteen and two-third (16 2-3) years. Why should Greensboro rent property at a monthly rental which would not pay for it under thirty years?

15. The question of the adequacy of the value of the land safely to secure the debt, and of the solvency or insolvency of the Southern Railway Company, would be neither presented to r decided by any court in such a case as the Southern Railway Company says will be brought.

This the 25th day of March, 1922.

THE COMMITTEE

In an age when the type, size, and style of a railroad station helped define the town, it was not uncommon for communities to promote and even fund the construction of bigger depots. Greensboro was no exception, and the community's support was instrumental in getting both the 1899 and the new depot built. In Greensboro, there was a small movement to block public funds from being used for a private enterprise.

Six

THE AWAITED ANNOUNCEMENT

The Tuesday, March 15, 1927, *Greensboro Record* heralded the awaited announcement: "First Train to Stop At Station on April 10." At that time, an announcement was made that no formal opening of the station was planned, although high-ranking Southern Railway officials were expected for the occasion. As it would turn out, the opening date was later changed to April 20.

On Wednesday, April 20, with the passing of Southern Railway's southbound Train No. 37, the Crescent, at 9:35 a.m., and a span of a few hours before any other trains were scheduled to arrive at the station, time was taken to transfer ticket offices; baggage, express, and mail department records; and stock to the new station. The first train scheduled to arrive in the new facility was to be Atlantic & Yadkin train No. 30 on its way east from Mt. Airy to Sanford and Wilmington, North Carolina, with a due time of 11:55 a.m. Train No. 45 was scheduled to be the first Southern Railway train to enter the station, with a scheduled time of 12:30 p.m. Shortly after, the Carolina Special from Goldsboro was due to arrive from the east, followed by northbound train No. 36. Along with the arrival of the trains, the new ticket office was scheduled to open at 11:00 a.m. J.E. Tomlinson, who as a younger man had attended the opening ceremonies for Southern Railway's station now being vacated on June 9, 1899, and who had bought the first ticket out of the old station, promised to be on time to buy the first ticket out of the new station. The announcement was made that the ticket office would be open around the clock, with a few exceptions. There were times when there was a lull in traffic and the facility could be closed without incident to passengers.

Like clockwork, the Atlantic & Yadkin Railway train from Mt. Airy was on time at 11:55 a.m. to take the honors as the first train to enter Greensboro's new station. The train was crewed by engineer N.M. Reynolds and conductor W.C. Donnell, a 40-year railroad veteran better known locally as "Cap'n Donnell," and was met by a number of Southern Railway officials, city officials, civic leaders, and citizenry who wanted to be present at the occasion. On the heels of the A&Y train, Southern train No. 4 from Winston-Salem arrived at 12:15 p.m. At 12:30 p.m., Southern train No. 45 entered the terminal, followed by northbound Southern Railway train No. 36 at 12:35 p.m. Shortly after, Southern train No. 21 westbound from Goldsboro arrived on its way to Asheville at 12:40 p.m. As necessitated by the track pattern in the station, train No. 21 backed into the station onto Track 2, and at the throttle were engineer G.S. Lane and conductor C.W. Fowler, both of Greensboro. As could be expected, throughout the day the station was thronged with not only legitimate passengers but also curious onlookers wanting to get a glimpse of the new station. Union News Company's stand and even the new barber shop and shoeshine stand were enjoying a brisk business. Each passenger arriving and leaving the new edifice was presented with flowers, a token of local florists who donated them for the occasion. By the end of the day, an estimated 10,000 people had thronged the station.

True to his word, promptly at 11:00 a.m., J.E. Tomlinson stepped up to the ticket office and bought his ticket on the next Winston-Salem–bound train. A.C. Lowrey Stafford was reported to be the second ticket purchaser headed for Terra Cotta, with both tickets sold by 20-year veteran Oscar F. York. Boarding the first outbound train, the Atlantic & Yadkin No. 30 bound for Sanford and Wilmington, North Carolina, was Mrs. T.J. Smith and her nephew. The first passenger to get off at the new station was J. Brown Evans of Fayetteville, having arrived on the same train No. 30 from Mt. Airy. The first woman passenger to alight from the first arriving A&Y train No. 30 into Greensboro was Margaret Ewing of Hollows, Virginia.

An interesting episode played out on Tuesday, April 26, just days after the new station opened. A porter who came in on train No. 135 became mystified by the new spacious depot and decided to take a closer look by going down the steps into the passenger subway beneath the tracks. Before he realized it and made a mad dash for his train, it was equally madly dashing out of the station on its way to Charlotte. An emergency wire was sent down the line to ready a fill-in porter to take his place. It was reported that since the station had opened, several Pullman conductors, as well as a number of passengers, had also wandered away too far and were left "while their charges were rolling to more distant points," as the paper put it.

In conjunction with the opening of the new station, on the morning of June 18, 1927, the first streetcar left the Southern Railway station at 6:15 a.m. to begin a regular 15-minute service from the station via Jefferson Square to Pomona.

As for the original 1899 Southern Railway Depot the new station was replacing, Southern Railway converted it into an office building for use as its division headquarters. On December 15, 1927, a fire consumed the top floor, causing a general alarm to be sounded by the fire department. Luckily, the firemen were able to quickly get the fire under control and save the building. The third floor and handsome turret were not replaced, but the building continued for decades as various railroad offices. At this writing, the 1899 depot has been purchased from Norfolk Southern by the North Carolina Railroad with the hope of restoring the vacant old building back to a useful structure.

This 1927 photograph shows that there is still some exterior work happening at the depot, but it is clear that construction is nearly complete. This iconic structure not only replaced the inadequate depot on Elm Street, but also housed mail, express freight, and a variety of railroad offices. (Courtesy of the Greensboro History Museum.)

Southeastern Express Company baggage carts sit on one of the passenger platforms at the station. Besides the six tracks serving the three passenger platforms, there are through tracks plus a number of tracks for switching and storage of express freight and extra passenger equipment.

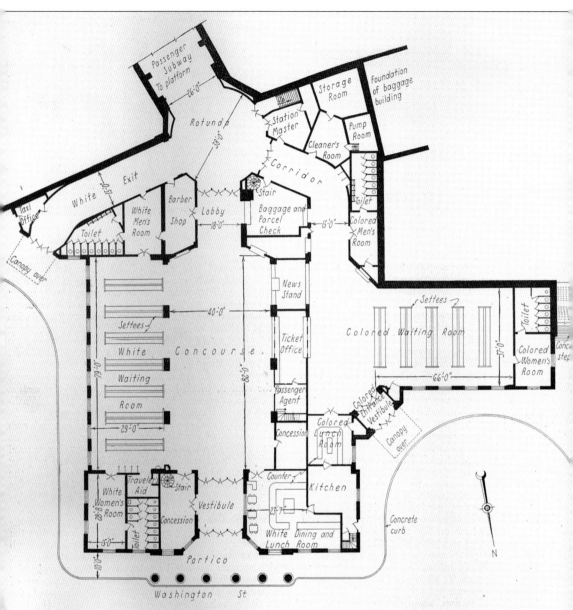

The Effective Layout of the New Station Provides Adequate Facilities for Both White and Colored Patrons

The April 1927 edition of *Railway Age* published the plan view of the main depot area. The plan clearly shows the segregated concourses that both led into the Rotunda and then through the tunnel to the platforms. With the Jim Crow laws of the South, the station had not only separate waiting areas, but also separate restrooms and lunchrooms. (Courtesy of *Railway Age*.)

Three steam engines and a variety of passenger equipment are shown at the passenger platforms and main station. Beyond the interesting trackwork, one of the water cranes is seen in the foreground, and there is another on the other end of the platforms. This view looks west toward Elm Street. (Courtesy of the Greensboro Chapter of the NRHS.)

This is the upper level of the depot at the mail loadout area. The depot's main entrance is to the left, at grade level with Washington Street. By the end of the 1920s, mail transported by the railroads peaked; however, mail transported by trains continued to be very important for both the railroads and the US Postal Service until the 1960s.

The skyline of Greensboro provides the backdrop for this 1935 photograph showing a Southern Railway 4-6-2, known as a Pacific Ps4, taking water from the water spigot on the east end of the Greensboro depot's platform. Painted green, Pacific steam engines were used as Southern Railway's premier passenger engines. (Both, courtesy of the Greensboro History Museum.)

This 1940s photograph shows the track side of the mail and express package parts of the depot. The first two cars are Railway Post Office (RPO)–baggage combinations, and the third car is a baggage car. It appears that these RPO cars are being pressed into service as additional baggage cars. (Courtesy of the Greensboro History Museum.)

This undated photograph shows a Southern Railway Ms-4 2-8-2, known as a Mikado, No. 4858, with a passenger train trailing behind. On the Southern Railway, Mikados—sometimes known as "MacArthurs" during World War II—mostly pulled freight trains. (Courtesy of the Greensboro History Museum.)

The main entrance to the segregated waiting room is pictured here. The Greensboro depot was built with substantial space dedicated to complying with segregation laws. Not only were there separate waiting rooms and restrooms, but also separate lunchrooms and access to vendors within the depot. Both waiting rooms emptied into the tunnel that led to the passenger platforms.

Contemporary maps label the doorway seen on the left as the "White Exit." Being built in 1927, the Southern Railway had to comply with segregation laws, also known as "Jim Crow laws." Restrooms, water fountains, waiting rooms, and even railroad coaches were all partitioned to keep the races separate.

The Berry family, along with what appear to be Sea Scouts, wait for the approaching train on one of the platforms in Greensboro sometime in 1942. During the war, many civic groups stepped up and provided supplementary services to offset the labor shortage. Both Scouts appear to be wearing their Eagle Scout medals. (Courtesy of Carol W. Martin and the Greensboro History Museum.)

With scores of passenger trains arriving and departing at the depot, passengers boarding a train was a common sight. The Berry family boards one of Southern Railway's passenger trains in 1942. Until recently, guests and non-passengers could wait on the platforms to greet or send off their friends and family. (Courtesy of Carol W. Martin and the Greensboro History Museum.)

THE PULLMAN COMPANY
PASSENGER'S CHECK—To identify accommodations purchased.

Greensboro to Washington, D. C.

LOWER BERTH............................CAR.............

LINE NO............................VIA............................R. R.
Property taken into car will be entirely at owner's risk.

OFFICE 18-16   FORM 26 $2.50

543

1 2 PERSONS

This is a Pullman sleeping berth ticket for a trip from Greensboro to Washington, DC, on April 21, 1934. The lower berth was the premium one on most trains, and a Pullman lower berth ticket was above the railroad's first-class ticket. As a perk, the lower berth sat facing forward while the upper berth passenger faced the back of the train. (Courtesy of the Greensboro Chapter of the NRHS.)

THE PULLMAN COMPANY
PASSENGER'S CHECK.
To be retained by passenger to identify accommodations indicated on the accompanying ticket. Property taken into car will be entirely at owner's risk. Subject to all other conditions stated on ticket.

NEW YORK to GREENSBORO

Lower
Berth No................ Car.............

Line No.............................

BK 12544

Rate $3.00

1395

No. Persons 1 2

When traveling by train over long distances, passengers could opt for more private and luxurious accommodations, including rooms with a bed. The sleeper cars were typically only added to mainline trains between big cities. This ticket is for a trip from New York City to Greensboro in a lower berth. (Courtesy of the Greensboro Chapter of the NRHS.)

ATLANTIC and YADKIN RAILWAY CO.

GREENSBORO, N. C.
—TO—
MOUNT AIRY, N. C.

Good for One Continuous Passage, commencing not later than o day after date of sale.

Subject to tariff regulations.

A L Thompson

Traffic Manager

PUGH, CIN'TI, O.

498F

The new 1927 depot's inaugural train was eastbound train No. 30 of the Atlantic & Yadkin Railway. The A&Y was a wholly owned subsidiary of the Southern but was run independently at the opening of the new station. This ticket is from May 1939 and is reportedly the last ticket sold for the last passenger train of the A&Y. (Courtesy of the Greensboro History Museum.)

A switch not properly routed to the mainline caused a terrific accident at the depot on July 20, 1941. Luckily, the coach track was empty when this big Mikado engine, No. 4907, ran out of track and crashed through the retaining wall, plummeting to the station's parking lot below. (Courtesy of Carol W. Martin and the Greensboro History Museum.)

Southern Railway class Ms-4 Mikado No. 4907 sits in the parking lot of the Greensboro depot on July 20, 1941. No. 4907 was built by Baldwin Locomotive Works in 1928 and was equipped with an Elesco water heater above the smokebox. Ms-4 class engines were the Southern Railway's standard mainline freight engines of the time. (Courtesy of the Greensboro History Museum.)

Crowds gather as Greensboro police officers salute the passing funeral train of Pres. Franklin D. Roosevelt on April 14, 1945. The president passed a couple of days before in Warm Springs, Georgia, and the train traveled first to Washington, DC, and then to Hyde Park, New York, over a three-day, nine-state journey. (Courtesy of Carol W. Martin and the Greensboro History Museum.)

Seven

DETAILING THE NEW
SOUTHERN RAILWAY STATION

Greensboro's new station when opened in 1927 was described as one of remarkable beauty. The first impression one had of this station was on the approach to its entrance. The six 26-foot-high limestone Roman Doric columns were impressive, and the station featured a Beaux-Arts façade consisting of a monumental Ionic portico with the six columns and a full entablature that screened a three-story arched entry. The redbrick structure with its limestone decorations made for a very pleasing and attractive station in its simple architectural beauty. The entrance opened directly into a vestibule with a floor of terrazzo marble design. Swinging oak doors led directly to the main concourse, with walls finished with Tennessee marble five feet high, the remainder being of cement plaster with a sand finish. The room was bordered on one side by a drug store and on the other by a café. The lobby and waiting room, some 31 by 86 feet, were combined, and the waiting room was furnished with large fumed oak benches to the right. On that same side were the ticket office windows, the Union News Company stand, and a Western Union telegraph station. The station was built with Neoclassical demilune windows and a large overhead mural that depicted the service area of the Southern Railway System. The station was described as fireproof throughout. Straight ahead was the underground passageway that led to the track entrances above. It was impressive, with its 192-foot length and 26-foot width. Over the passageway was a large clock so necessary in a train station. Over the clock, a large 14-by-9-foot color map was installed depicting the United States, with special emphasis given to the lines owned and operated by Southern Railway outlined in a conspicuous red. An annunciator board was located prominently near the entrance to the rotunda and the subway passage to the trains. On either side of the passageway were a barbershop and other necessary establishments. Leading from the left of the main underground passageway was a smaller passageway leading to a large court used for parking. As was the custom of the era, a separate waiting room for Black passengers was to the right of the main lobby and waiting room. In front of this waiting room were the ticket offices, newsstand, and telegraph office. Leading from the large underground passage was a series of steps up to the broad butterfly platforms and the trains. There was a long ramp to reach the mainline's two tracks. The second platform, which was slightly shorter than the main one, had steps that led to the tracks used by the Goldsboro, Winston-Salem, and Asheville Division trains. The third platform area, which was a bit shorter than the second one, was used by trains of the Atlantic & Yadkin Railway. On the same level as the railroad tracks above and adjoining the station proper were large rooms for the baggage, express, and mail departments. Access to these facilities was through Eckles Street, which opened into a broad paved area surrounding those departments.

The track layout at the station was well arranged and complete and was pronounced excellent by those who knew. Every train could pull in quickly and directly into the station and leave the same way. A double-track mainline opened from the north and west into the eight station tracks, six of which were utilized for passenger trains, while two were for freight trains passing through Greensboro on the mainline. The six passenger tracks were served by three island platforms: two tracks to a platform. The platform nearest the station was the longest of the three and was used primarily by trains operating through Greensboro on the main Southern Railway line north to

Danville and Washington and south to Charlotte and Atlanta. It was some 1,200 feet long, able to accommodate up to a 16-car train. Of special interest was the width of this platform. It was 22 feet wide, in contrast to the other two platforms, which were only 17 feet wide. The center platform housing two tracks was 1,000 feet in length and used primarily by North Carolina Division or Goldsboro–Winston-Salem and Asheville trains. The third platform was only 700 feet in length and was used mostly for the shorter trains of the A&Y. Between the passenger platforms and the station building were five additional tracks. The one nearest the station building was used strictly for baggage, mail, and express cars. The other four, with a 26-car capacity, were used to store similar cars that routinely were added and taken off at this important railroad junction. Just to the east of the station were two spur tracks for the express purpose of parking private railroad officials' cars and dining cars added or taken off at Greensboro. The station platforms were six inches above the rail level. Whereas the mainline rails were laid with 100-pound rail, in the station, they were 85 pounds and laid on untreated ties in stone ballast. In making the track changes in connection with the building of the new station and the accompanying required underpasses, Southern Railway had to go to considerate expense. Significant effort was involved in raising the mainline tracks some three feet at the Elm-Davie underpass and one foot at the Washington Street underpass. These changes made a one-half percent grade from the west as far as Elm Street. From there, the grade was a full percent leading into the station, three-tenths of one percent through the station, and then one percent down until the original grade was reached north of Washington Street. The only criticism directed at the station track arrangement was the way the entrance by incoming Goldsboro trains, which had to make a time-consuming maneuver of backing into the station. This was necessitated by the location of the Sergeant Manufacturing Company plant at the angle between Southern Railway's mainline and the Goldsboro branch line.

This is the main concourse as seen from the main entrance. The large system map can be seen above the doorway leading to the passenger tunnel that connected the depot with the platforms. The main arrival board can be seen to the left. By the time this photograph was taken on March 22, 1977, many amenities in the station had closed. (Courtesy of Mike Small.)

This image is looking from the rotunda into the passenger tunnel on July 31, 1976. The tunnel allowed safe access beneath the busy mainlines of the Southern without the passengers having to cross the tracks at grade. (Courtesy of Mike Small.)

This March 3, 1978, photograph shows the main concourse facing Washington Street before the arrival of one of the Southern Crescent trains. People are lined up at the ticket counter. Note the old baggage cart still in use. The arched windows on the left are blacked out with paint, a wartime measure to conceal light at night. (Courtesy of Mike Small.)

With the baggage car closest to the photographer, a string of lightweight aluminum passenger cars attached to train No. 2, the Southern Crescent, wait for their northbound departure early on the morning of November 27, 1976. The Crescent normally arrived at the depot at 2:15 a.m. (Courtesy of Mike Small.)

From the tunnel to the platforms are ramps that branch off. Looking from inside the tunnel, the doorway to the access ramp to Tracks 1 and 2 is propped open. To the right is the view looking from the platform to the tunnel. Note the exit sign labeling Tracks 1 and 2. Unfortunately, the old signage did not survive the station renovations. These photographs were taken on July 30, 1976. (Both, courtesy of Mike Small.)

This was the view looking down the ramp on July 30, 1976, toward the tunnel that took passengers under the mainline to the depot. The ramp made it easy for passengers to get from the depot to the platforms. (Courtesy of Mike Small.)

The arrival board at the station, dated July 31, 1976, shows Southern Railway's passenger service in its waning days. On February 1, 1979, Amtrak, which started a little over five years before, took over the Crescent from the Southern Railway—one of the last railroads to make the change. (Courtesy of Mike Small.)

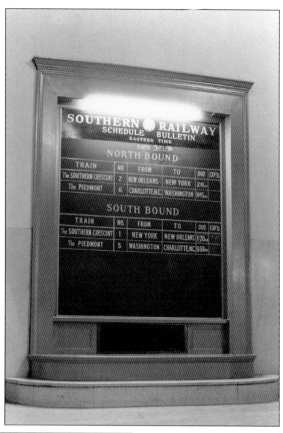

By the late 1960s, the railroad struggled with finding affordable accommodations for its crews. This former Pullman sleeper car, No. 5400, was pressed into service as a dormitory car to house passenger train employees overnight in Greensboro in about July 1963.

From 1947 to 1949, the first Freedom Train traveled the continental United States, visiting all 48 states. On December 5, 1947, the Freedom Train visited Greensboro depot and a little girl is being interviewed by a radio announcer from WBIG. In the background is one of the 29 US Marines assigned guard duty for the train. (Courtesy of Carol W. Martin and the Greensboro History Museum.)

These passengers have just debarked from the Southern Crescent in March 1978 and are waiting for their rides outside the front entrance of the depot as taxicabs line up. At this time, the Southern Crescent was still a Southern Railway passenger train, and one of the last non-Amtrak long-distance trains—something that would change early the next year. (Courtesy of Mike Small.)

This undated photograph looks north up Elm Street as one of Southern Railway's Alco S-1 switch engines shunts a passenger coach from the depot. The Clegg Hotel, on the left, catered to rail passengers and was located next to the 1899 depot.

The northbound Southern Crescent, sitting in light snow, is ready to depart Greensboro on February 22, 1978. Engine 6905 is an E8A and is painted green and white. Below, the same engine is seen heading southbound on July 31, 1976, running late, as train No. 1 on the bridge over Davie Street. The second engine in the consist is No. 6900, which is currently preserved at the NC Transportation Museum in Spencer, North Carolina. (Both, courtesy of Mike Small.)

Eight

ADDITIONAL
STATION FACILITIES

Connected to the station by a concrete platform and shed, the new commodious quarters of the Southeastern Express Company were in a two-story redbrick building at the western end of the station. The lower floor on the level with the station platforms was 50 feet wide by 172 feet long, while the upper story was the same width but 61 feet long. The lower story housed storage rooms and the check-in office, while the upper story was used for administrative offices. J.R. Sowell was the head man in the Greensboro operation, supervising some 60 personnel. About 50 express messengers were in and out of the facility every day or so.

In the new station, passenger convenience was primary, and the handling of baggage by the railroad staff was a bit more difficult. A passenger with ticket in hand and no baggage to check could make a straight dash from the front doors to the subway leading to the tracks. More difficulty was had getting baggage to and from the trains that were much farther away than at the old facility. There was another difficulty in having to transfer baggage from one train to another, in that there were three platforms and six tracks to be considered.

Also in the westernmost area of the new station on track level were the spacious quarters for the US Postal Service. Heading the operation as senior transfer clerk was P.D. Whitehead. His staff's responsibilities included seeing that the mail sacks leaving the post office were placed on the wagons that were rolled to the right train. All mail destined for Greensboro had to be brought to the loading platform where waiting post office trucks would carry it to the main post office.

In charge of all station concessions, including the restaurant, soda fountain, drugstore, bookstore, newsstand, and novelties, as well as the barber shop and shoeshine parlor, was J.H. Lamon, a Washington, DC, resident and newcomer to Greensboro who became the superintendent in charge of all operations for the Union News Company. The restaurant had eight tables with a 32-patron seating capacity, along with 26 counter stools, which brought the total to 58. Separate facilities for Blacks provided a counter with 20 stools. C.L. Stubberfield oversaw both restaurants. A marble soda fountain with candies, toilet goods, over-the-counter medicine, and tobacco was at the front to the left of the main entrance. This was to the right of where the restaurant was positioned. This restaurant was perhaps the Union News Company's chief pride with its marble walls and shining brass and marble fixtures in the center. On the left in the rear of the waiting room was a three-chair barbershop operated by W.J. Smith. In the barbershop was a shoeshine bench. Two separate units on the right of the waiting room contained the book, magazine, and fruit stands. On the station's second-floor opening onto the tracks was a terminal for 35 Union News agents who would be dispatched to sell the company's wares on trains traveling north as far as Washington, south to Atlanta, and east to Raleigh, Wilmington, and Florence, South Carolina. Union News Company had expended some $50,000 to provide handsome oak fixtures.

Travelers' aid was not forgotten in the new station, with ample facilities provided to assist those needing help. A participating agency of the Greensboro Community Chest (now known as the United Way), was provided space.

Ample space was allotted for cabs in the plaza courts flanking the station. W.J. Wyrick, manager for the Yellow Cab Company of Greensboro, assured that his people would meet every arriving train. In the event someone needed a cab outside of train hours, a call to him would bring a cab to the station immediately.

Above, a Railway Express Agency (REA) motorized cart sits on one of the passenger platforms ready to unload its cargo. The below photograph shows an REA employee driving the small, motorized cart, loaded with a substantial lockbox. The REA occupied a sizeable building attached to the depot. That space allowed for the transloading of goods from rail to truck for local delivery, or for pickup. (Both, courtesy of the Greensboro Chapter of the NRHS.)

An REA tractor with a long string of carts—all loaded with tires—sits on the north-side passenger platform. The REA handled a variety of express shipments, from baked goods to home goods. The REA was jointly owned by several railroads, including the Southern Railway. (Courtesy of the Greensboro Chapter of the NRHS.)

The reverse side of a shipping tag from the REA advertises the company's contribution to the war effort during World War II. (Courtesy of the Greensboro Chapter of the NRHS.)

Railway Express Company carts are stored three deep in front of the Railway Express Building in this 1959 photograph. A Southern Railway baggage car sits with its door open behind the carts. In the photograph below are a Railway Express Company tow motor and, in the distance, one of its delivery trucks. (Both, courtesy of the Greensboro History Museum.)

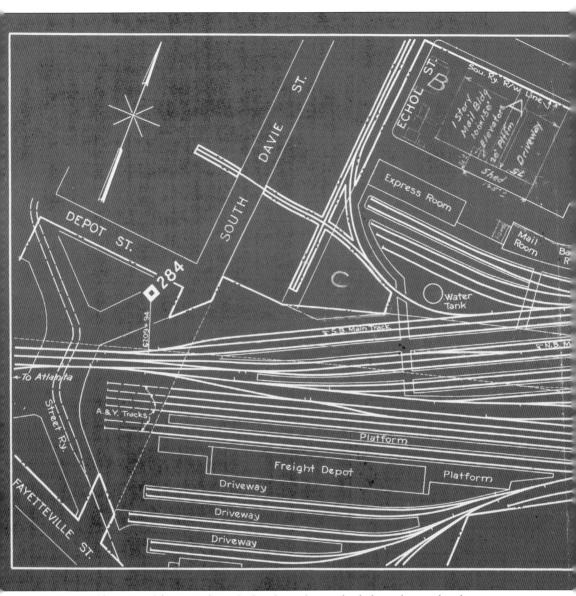

Labels visible on blueprint: ECHOL ST., SOUTH DAVIE ST., DEPOT ST., 284, To Atlanta, Street Ry., A. & Y. Tracks, FAYETTEVILLE ST., Freight Depot, Driveway, Driveway, Driveway, Platform, Platform, Water Tank, Express Room, Mail Room, Ba R, Sou. Ry. R/W Line, 1 Story Mail Bldg., Elevators, Shed, Driveway, S. Ns. Main Track, S. Bd. Main track, A, B, C

This 1946 blueprint of the station's track plan shows five tracks dedicated to mail and express agency loading and unloading. In addition to the main depot and express agency building, this plan also

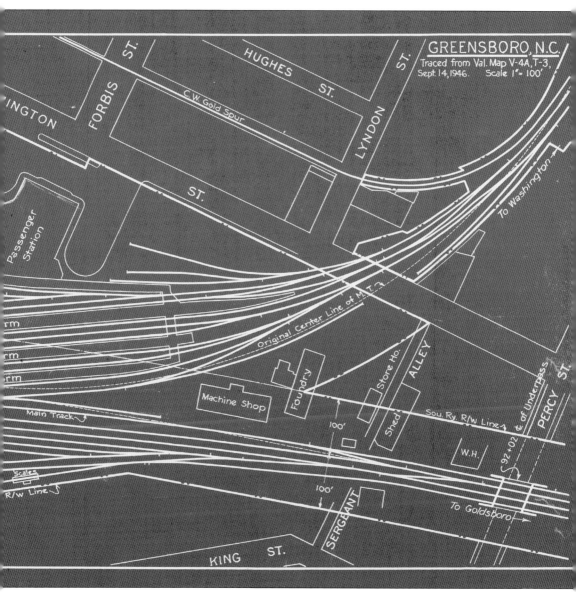

shows the one-story mail building erected on Washington Street in front of the express building.

Marks on the platform, and even the baggage cart's wheels, allow for ease of transloading. Arriving trains have specific stopping places to accommodate consistent passenger, mail, and baggage loading. This cart is labeled for the Southeastern Express, a predecessor of the Railway Express Agency. (Courtesy of the Greensboro Chapter of the NRHS.)

Pictured is the Railway Express Agency building, with the office to the right and the warehouse and shops to the left. Today, this building houses the Greyhound bus terminal in the old office portion and the Carolina Model Railroaders and the Greensboro Chapter of the National Railway Historical Society in the warehouse end.

Seen here is another view of the Railway Express Agency building. The sign hanging in front of the closed roll-up door proclaims, "Fast Service Shipping Terminals." According to interviews with former employees, the REA building also housed a company blacksmith shop.

Express companies were nationalized during World War I into the American Railway Express Agency, which survived until 1929, when control was returned to the railroads. The new Railway Express Agency was jointly owned by 86 railroads. In between, the Southern Railway partially owned the Southeastern Express Agency, which occupied part of the depot until the REA replaced it.

The 1953 Greensboro Railway Express Agency baseball team stands in front of one of its express trucks with an RJ Reynolds Camel cigarettes ad. While the players are unidentified, the man in the suit at left is Bruce Fowler. (Courtesy of the Greensboro Chapter of the NRHS.)

Nine

In Summary

At its peak, 42 passenger trains a day passed through Greensboro's Southern Railway Station portals. This was greatly increased in busy periods when certain trains had to be operated with an additional or even two additional sections. World War II brought troop trains that passed through Greensboro, further increasing the strain on the station's capacity. Like all other American railroad centers, a major decline commenced in passenger train usage after the war. In May 1979, the last Southern Railway train passed through the station, and the building was donated by the railroad to the City of Greensboro. Until 2005, Amtrak passengers were served from rented facilities owned by Norfolk Southern Railway out of a freight office in Pomona, several miles west of downtown Greensboro on Oakland Avenue. Beginning in 1993, the progressive North Carolina Department of Transportation and the City of Greensboro both began to push for the return of passenger service to the original station and to improve connections with local and area bus lines and intercity carriers, creating a true intermodal facility for Greensboro.

Restoration of the station commenced, including the reconfiguration of a portion of the tracks near the station, extending the original passenger tunnel, and the building of a new baggage tunnel, boarding platforms, and canopy sheds for the convenience of the passengers. Additional modernization included trackside escalators and digital arrival and departure monitors. Despite all the modernization, significant effort was made to retain the original 1920s appearance.

Phase one of construction began in the summer of 2001 and was completed in the summer of 2003. Crews restored the lower passenger areas and converted the upper-level baggage handling areas to waiting areas for Greensboro Transit Authority city buses as well as the area's Piedmont Authority for Regional Transit buses. The building that originally served the Southeastern Railway Express Company and later the Railway Express Company now began to house intercity bus services. Greyhound began operations from the terminal in August 2003. During phase two, crews worked on the interior of the depot for Amtrak services; reconstructed the pedestrian tunnel, passenger platforms, and sheds; and constructed the new baggage tunnel. All work was completed in October 2005. The Federal Transit Administration, Federal Highway Administration, and state and city funds paid for the $32 million project that created Greensboro's intermodal facility.

J. Douglas Galyon Sr., a Greensboro civic leader and textile executive and 17-year member of the North Carolina Board of Transportation, advocated for the depot's return to service. With the station's reopening in 2005, the past chairman of the transportation board was honored by having the 1927 station named the J. Douglas Galyon Depot.

At this writing, the station is served by three Amtrak trains: the *Crescent*, operating between New York, Washington, Atlanta, Birmingham, and New Orleans; the *Carolinian*, between Charlotte, Washington, and New York City; and the *Piedmont*, with multiple trains between Charlotte and Raleigh, North Carolina—in all, 10 passenger trains a day. For the year 2017, a total of 111,187 passengers entrained at Greensboro.

The future for Greensboro's J. Douglas Galyon Depot is assured.

On October 10, 1960, US senator Lyndon B. Johnson steps off the train in Greensboro while on a whistle-stop campaign tour, part of the John F. Kennedy ticket that would win the White House that year. (Courtesy of the Edward J. McCauley Photographic Materials [P0082], North Carolina Collection Photographic Archives, Wilson Special Collections Library, University of North Carolina at Chapel Hill.)

Large crowds gathered at the depot to hear Senator Johnson speak in the parking lot. Johnson's stop in Greensboro was part of a campaign by train through the South that was instrumental in helping Kennedy win. (Both, courtesy of the Edward J. McCauley Photographic Materials [P0082], North Carolina Collection Photographic Archives, Wilson Special Collections Library, University of North Carolina at Chapel Hill.)

A one-story mail facility was built at street level in front of the express building to help with the volume of mail. Additional mail sorting structures were eventually needed. Below is an open shed used for the transloading of mail from trains. Both photographs are from January 1962.

This bleak photograph from 1972 highlights the decline of passenger services at the depot. One of the passenger platform's umbrella shelters has been removed to accommodate larger freight cars. The Southern Railway faced this issue as early as 1942 and solved it by cutting back the butterfly passenger sheds at a cost of $2,000. This continuing problem made removal an attractive solution.

This 1970s photograph shows a door that was cut into a window opening in what was the segregated waiting room. The room was used by the Carolina Model Railroaders for their model train layout from the mid-1970s until the renovation in 2001. Today, they share space with the Greensboro Chapter of the NRHS in the old express building.

Formed in 1973, Carolina Model Railroaders rented space at the depot from Southern Railway. That lease was continued by the city after the railroad donated the depot to Greensboro. The club built a large, nationally recognized scale layout in the space. Since 2003, the model railroad club has occupied a large portion of the former express building next door. (Photograph by Mac Connery; courtesy of Carolina Model Railroaders.)

Passengers board an Amtrak train at the Pomona Yard depot in August 1985. When the Southern Railway gave up passenger service in 1979, the stop was moved to Oakland Avenue. The Pomona depot, which served until 2005, was spartan, with a small waiting room and no passenger sheds. (Photograph by Gene Kirkman, courtesy of the Greensboro Chapter of the NRHS.)

Remnants of the past lay in ruins as remodeling transfers the single tunnel to the platforms into two tunnels: one for passengers and one for baggage and Amtrak personnel. Normally buried, this shot shows the deck girder bridge for the line that heads north. The tunnel renovation was part of the second phase of the depot project. (Courtesy of R. Bruce Smith.)

Concrete debris and cut-up steel girders litter the tunnel as part of the 2001 renovation. The tunnel was "daylighted" as part of the remodeling to allow for a new ceiling structure. The alcoves seen here once held wooden benches; their outlines can be seen in the aqua accent paint. (Courtesy of R. Bruce Smith.)

119

A modern tracked excavator, a Komatsu PC 300 LC, locally owned by D.H. Griffin Wrecking Company, works on the tunnel renovation and expansion. Extensive work was completed on the tunnel to make it safe and efficient for the rebirth of the passenger station. (Courtesy of R. Bruce Smith.)

The renovated depot's namesake, J. Douglas Galyon, was a longtime civic leader and 10-year member of the North Carolina Board of Transportation, with most of that time spent as the board chairman. Galyon is seen here speaking at the grand opening of the depot on October 21, 2005. (Courtesy of the Galyon family.)

J. Douglas Galyon is pictured at the ribbon cutting and grand opening of the depot named after him on October 21, 2005. The depot underwent a major renovation, restoring it as Greensboro's passenger station. Additionally, the building was designed to become a transportation hub serving Greyhound buses along with city and regional bus lines. (Courtesy of the Galyon family.)

J. Douglas Galyon (center), along with Congressman Howard Coble, Mayor Keith Holliday, North Carolina senator Kay Hagen, Congressman Mel Watt, and others, cut the ribbon at the grand opening of Greensboro's J. Douglas Galyon Depot. Mayor Holliday stated during the event that Galyon's leadership helped Greensboro remain the Gate City. (Courtesy of the Galyon family.)

Passengers wait to board the Norfolk & Western 611. Special excursion trips regularly departed from Greensboro, and before 4:30 a.m. on April 23, 2016, the lines already were formed. The Virginia Transportation Museum—owners of the 611—enlisted the aid of the Greensboro Chapter of the NRHS and the Carolina Model Railroaders to help facilitate the boarding process. (Courtesy of the Greensboro Chapter of the NRHS.)

Long lines formed out the door and around the parking lot in the very early morning hours of April 23, 2016, as two days of special steam excursion trains departed the restored depot. The excursions featured the Norfolk and Western 611 and luxurious private passenger cars traveling from Greensboro to Roanoke, Virginia, and back. (Courtesy of the Greensboro Chapter of the NRHS.)

Food for one of the Norfolk & Western 611 excursions has been loaded onto an Amtrak shuttle cart to be carried underground to the station's platform. The main concourse is connected to all of the depot's platforms exclusively through tunnels, with train access by way of escalator, stairs, and elevator. (Courtesy of the Greensboro Chapter of the NRHS.)

The Virginia Transportation Museum's steam excursion train sits at the Greensboro Depot's platform awaiting passengers. The train consisted of various privately held coaches, dome cars, and dining cars. During the remodel, the old umbrella-style platform sheds were removed and replaced with larger ones designed to accommodate the taller freight cars that pass through Greensboro. (Courtesy of the Greensboro Chapter of the NRHS.)

Part of the boarding crew that helped with the steam excursion in 2016, provided by the members of the Carolina Model Railroaders, stands in front of the large Southern Railway system map in the main concourse. During the renovations, the City of Greensboro was careful to preserve many of the original features of the depot. (Courtesy of the Greensboro Chapter of the NRHS.)

US senator Barack Obama shakes hands with some of an 18,000-person crowd at a presidential campaign stop in front of the depot on September 27, 2008. The future president was accompanied by his running mate and also future president, US senator Joe Biden. (Courtesy of Jack Sinclair.)

Pictured is a ticket to the "Change We Need" rally held on the grounds of the J. Douglas Galyon Depot. This was not the first campaign "stump speech" to be held at the depot, but it probably is the largest rally ever held there. (Courtesy of Jack Sinclair.)

Above, Norfolk Southern Railway yardmaster Jim Lawrence (far left) and trainmaster Dwight Anderson (standing) teach conductor trainees. Below, in 2016, the railroad utilized the Carolina Model Railroaders' model train layout to help its trainees better understand the building of trains and blocking of railcars. The simulated exercise using HO-scale trains and representations of local railyards was a success, and nearly 100 trainees passed through the club program. (Both, courtesy of the Greensboro Chapter of the NRHS.)

Built to handle high volumes of passenger traffic, the depot survived the decline of passenger service and then closed as a passenger station. It endured decades of decay, teen discos, and vagrants, to be reborn. With passenger trains arriving many times a day, the multimodal J. Douglas Galyon Depot's future is secure. (Courtesy of Jack Sinclair.)

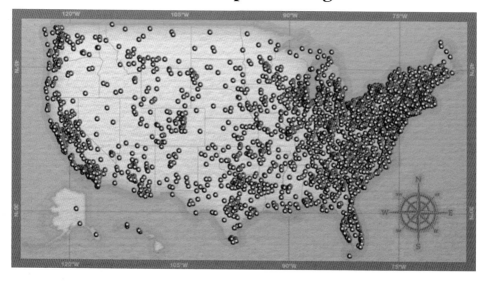